NEW YORK'S
ONE-FOOD
WONDERS

A GUIDE TO THE BIG APPLE'S
UNIQUE SINGLE-FOOD
SPOTS

NEW YORK'S ONE-FOOD WONDERS

A GUIDE TO THE BIG APPLE'S UNIQUE SINGLE-FOOD SPOTS

MITCH BRODER

Photography by Jai Williams

Globe Pequot

Guilford, Connecticut

In memory of Mindie

Globe
Pequot

An imprint of Rowman & Littlefield
Distributed by NATIONAL BOOK NETWORK

Copyright © 2015 by Mitch Broder
Photographs © 2015 by Jai Williams

British Library Cataloguing in Publication Information Available

Library of Congress Cataloging-in-Publication Data Available

ISBN 978-1-4930-0642-7 (paperback)
ISBN 978-1-4930-1741-6 (e-book)

∞™ The paper used in this publication meets the minimum requirements of American National Standard for Information Sciences—Permanence of Paper for Printed Library Materials, ANSI/NISO Z39.48-1992.

CONTENTS

ACKNOWLEDGMENTS

The joy of this project, besides eating everything I ate, was talking to the people who made the project possible. As I point out in the introduction, this is not just a book about food, it's a book about passion. In pursuing their passions, these people gave me one of my own.

So thanks to the owners, founders, managers, and occasional spokespeople who gave their time to tell me what I needed to know. And thanks to everyone who plays a part in peppering New York City with culinary concepts that are delicious in more ways than one.

Thanks to my editor, Amy Lyons, for having the confidence in me to say yes before I even finished explaining the idea. Thanks to my agent, Anne Marie O'Farrell, of the Marcil-O'Farrell literary agency, for always keeping me grounded, whether I want to be or not.

This book follows the success of *Discovering Vintage New York*, and the best part of that success has been the support of good friends. Special thanks to Rick Allen, Jeanne Chamas, the Greenhill family, Jeff Mangum, Debbi Porterfield, Lydia Ruth, Hank Shaw, and Mary Shustack.

Thanks to the writers and reporters who have covered that first book and to the many people who have come to the events for that book. And thanks to the talented people of Globe Pequot Press, who designed, edited, publicized, marketed, and otherwise cared for that book.

Loving thanks to my father, King Broder, who always believes that I'll succeed. And loving thanks to Patricia Greenhill, who is not only the light of my life, but also the chef of my life. Without her coaxing, I probably wouldn't have started this book, and without her cooking, I probably wouldn't have lived long enough to finish it.

INTRODUCTION

New York is where you go to make it on your own. Especially if you're a single food.

Dominating a menu is tough to start with. And if you're, say, a peanut-butter sandwich, it's just that much tougher. You need a city with people enough not only to seek out a peanut-butter sandwich, but also to presume that, as a dominator, you're one bodacious peanut-butter sandwich.

That city is New York—which starts out with around 8 million people and in annual visitors adds around 50 million more. Those people are enough to sustain not only a peanut-butter-sandwich restaurant but also, as it happens, an ice-cream-sandwich restaurant.

New York is a single-food paradise, and for more than those millions of reasons. It's unbeatable for walking. It's unmatchable for exploring. Consequently, it's unquenchable for restaurants that are unimaginable. No wonder it made peanut butter think it could make it on its own.

The city has amassed scores of places that feature one food, and those places were getting hungry to be featured in one guide. They needed a book that would tell everyone about them all—and all about them. Here it is. I hope they appreciate it. I hope it takes you to paradise.

I was the right one to write it, because I'm obsessed with these places. I've been writing about them for over a quarter of a century. I've covered everything from the still-flourishing all-peanut-butter restaurant to the fallen all-blintz and all-potato-chip restaurants. My obsession is not just with food, though it's considerably with food. It's also with faith, moxie, and monumental improbability. I'm not at all sure that peanut butter had any better odds than blintzes, but I am sure that their respective restaurateurs scoffed at the odds.

This is my second book. The first was *Discovering Vintage New York,* which covers the restaurants and shops that have survived for at least 50 years. *New York's One-Food Wonders* might seem like a curious follow-up. But it's actually the perfect companion. These spots are the other vintage. Most lack a vintage look, since most aren't very old. But most have a vintage spirit, since that's what got them here. In a cityscape nearly eclipsed by multiple links of monotonous chains, these places collectively stand as a bastion of individuality and guts.

Of course, the one-food trend was hot even two centuries ago, when the city was rife with oyster cellars, oyster saloons, and oyster stands. By the late 1800s, pushcart vendors were pushing specialties including sausages, hot dogs, chestnuts, peanuts, and New York pretzels.

Today the food at a one-food restaurant is most likely to be hamburgers, subs, tacos, pizza, or covertly named fried chicken. This book takes you to the less likely food. In here you find restaurants with names like OatMeals, Porchetta, Caracas Arepa Bar, and Caviar Russe. You'll find the spot that sells gourmet chicken fingers, the spots that sell Australian meat pies, and the Home of the Original Meatball in a Cup. You'll find a few places that sell grilled cheese, a couple that sell mac and cheese, and one that sells everything it can think of with cheese.

I've included an occasional chain if it sells something that's unusual, and I've included conventional foods when they're not typically found on their own. But for the most part, I've included the places that the cover promises: the city's *unique* single-food spots. The one-food *wonders*.

I've frequently spotlighted the people behind the places, because their stories are often at least as fascinating as their food. So this book is not only a New York City food guide, but also a collection of New York City stories, not to mention a potential motivational bestseller.

What's more, it transcends food. Though focused on one-food wonders, it has a section chronicling the city's one-*thing* wonders. If a place that's dependent on selling meals made of oatmeal belongs in a book, I reasoned, so does a place that's dependent on selling books about Winston Churchill.

I've further included the first New York Singular Hall of Fame, in recognition of the plucky quests of the past. It celebrates spots fondly remembered along with those long forgotten. This is probably the only book that will ever recall a place called HOTPUFFS.

Still, the vast majority of this book's dozens of stories are about currently available food. They explain the food's concept. They often explain the food's origin. They sometimes explain how the food is eaten. They occasionally explain what the food is.

They usually don't include the food's prices. If they did, you still wouldn't know them. New York City food is a victim of chronic price creep. But a decent portion at most of these places will run you around 5 to 15 bucks. I trusted that you wouldn't want to read that a hundred or so times.

At those prices, you could say that this is a book about cheap eats. But it isn't that to me. To me, it's a book about passion. It's about the passion of people who took big risks to follow delectable dreams. It's about the passion that all of us can have for delectable foods. It's also, like my first book, about a changing city—a city where price creep of a bigger sort is especially tough on dreams. Opening a tiny shop selling french fries gets more and more practical as closing a restaurant in the face of tripling rent gets more and more common.

I've urged people to visit the vintage spots before it's too late. But I've never called for a boycott of new spots (though some of them seem to ask for it). The places in this book—a few of which are vintage—bring adventure to the city, and adventure is what the city is in danger of losing.

The best reward for my first book has been hearing from people who say that it's guided them to some of their best memories of New York. So have your opinions about the implications and ramifications of the places in this book. But first have a peanut-butter sandwich.

THE CITY'S BEST ONE-FOOD WONDERS

A SALT & BATTERY

112 Greenwich Ave., New York, NY 10011
(212) 691-2713   asaltandbattery.com

BRITISH INVASION

For your best deal on a trip to England, take the subway to 14th Street, then walk a block to Greenwich Avenue and then be gobsmacked. Your trip costs subway fare, and you have everything you need: an English restaurant, an English food shop, and a chippy, with an edgy name. The chippy's name is A Salt & Battery, since it's the kind of chippy that offers fried seafood and potatoes, better known as fish-and-chips. And it's a genuine chippy, since it's the work of two genuine Brits who've been colonizing the avenue since the early '90s.

Nicky Perry claimed the territory in 1991 with Tea & Sympathy, a restaurant that, besides tea, offers English comfort food. She followed that with Carry On Tea & Sympathy, an English food and takeout shop, and in 1999 opened A Salt, for a working-class touch.

Along the way, she married Sean Kavanagh-Dowsett, who now rules the British empire with her. A Salt, Sean says, preserves a fading tradition. Even in England, he says, "pure fish-and-chips shops are getting fewer and farther between." He calls A Salt "a best exemplar," and it's pretty close to pure.

It offers pollock, haddock, sole, whiting, shrimp, scallops, or cod, battered and deep-fried to the proper golden brown. It offers chips, which are neither potato chips nor french fries, but—well, chips. And it offers other traditional sides like Heinz Baked Beans and mushy peas. With the genuine foods, it sells genuine drinks, like Idris Fiery Ginger Beer, R White's Premium

Lemonade, and Boddington's Pub Ale. And its star dessert is a battered, deep-fried English Mars bar, which is different from an American Mars bar, and even more so when it's fried.

You can dine among artifacts like a picture from Charles and Diana's wedding and an autographed Albert Square sign from the British soap *EastEnders*, while listening to British radio stations playing British classics like "I Only Want to Be With You" by Dusty Springfield.

If you want to make a contest of it, enter the delicately titled I'm a Big Fat Ba$t@rd Challenge. Buy a pound of fish and a pound and a half of chips, down them in 20 minutes or less, and get a refund along with a T-shirt. Listen, it used to be two pounds of chips. And if you want to make a night of it, rent the restaurant's genuine London taxicab. It's a stately black 1980 Austin FX4D. It's known for turning heads around the city, which is why they may not let you have it if you've just taken the Big Fat Ba$t@rd Challenge.

There's definitely British wit at work throughout this little kingdom, and it's been working since Nicky first opened the door of Tea & Sympathy. That's a charming place—but a tiny place. It seats at best 23, and it's popular. So on the door Nicky posted Nicky's Rules. They include the rule to wait outside until your whole group has arrived, and the rule to "naff off" after you've eaten, if people are waiting. "People think, 'Those rules can't possibly apply to me,'" Sean says, "and those tend to be the people they apply to the most."

Those who obey get to indulge in English culinary classics from tea and scones to bangers and mash to tweed kettle pie. Those who don't can go next door and stock up on English culinary classics like Tunnock's Tea Cakes, Marmite Yeast Extract, and Milkybar Buttons. Or they can go another door down to A Salt & Battery, where the biggest rule is the time limit on the Big Fat challenge. Which doesn't mean that the food is any less good, Sean makes clear: "We're of the school of thought that if you can't do it absolutely right, don't do it at all."

ASIA DOG

66 Kenmare St., New York, NY 10012

(212) 226-8861   asiadognyc.com

CONTINENTAL CUISINE

If you've wondered why your own grilled hot dogs have never paid off, it's undoubtedly because they're just not worldly enough. Pick a continent. Make hot dogs that are inspired by that continent. Before long, you should have your own hot-dog store. Don't complain if you picked Antarctica.

Steve and Melanie Porto picked Asia, and they got their own hot-dog store, to which they gave the pragmatic name of Asia Dog. It has dogs inspired by China, Japan, Korea, Thailand, and Vietnam. But the dogs weren't invented for a store. They were invented for a yard. "Our friends have a bar called Trophy Bar, and they were opening the backyard," Melanie says. "They asked Steve to grill hot dogs and hamburgers to bring people in. He wanted to do a twist on traditional hot dogs, and being Korean, he had always eaten kimchi on his."

He made Korean dogs and Chinese dogs and Vietnamese dogs, and the couple ended up cooking at Trophy every Tuesday. They cooked at other bars on other nights, at the Brooklyn Flea market on weekends, and at Central Park Summerstage in summer. A store was their destiny.

It opened in 2011, three years after the barbecue. Today the top dog on its menu is the one called the Mel and Steve. It's made with Asian sesame slaw, scallions, and sesame seeds. Steve is half Korean, and Mel is half Chinese, so their namesake, Melanie says, is "half Asian and half Caucasian."

For all-Chinese, you get the Wangding, made with barbecued pork belly, cucumber, and scallions. For all-Korean, it's the Ginny, with kimchi and nori flakes. ("Wangding" is Mel and Steve's fusion of two Chinese friends' last names. Ginny is a Korean friend who "puts kimchi on everything.") The Vietnamese dog has pork pâté, spicy aioli, cucumber, pickled carrot and

daikon, jalapeño, and cilantro. The Japanese dog has Japanese curry and kimchi apples. The Thai dog has mango relish and crushed peanuts. The American dog has ketchup and mustard.

Your dog can be beef, chicken, vegetarian, or organic beef; your bun can be white or whole wheat. If you're not a dog person, you can choose a similarly influenced burger or salad. If you're a hard-core dog person, you can choose the kimchi pancake corn dog.

Asia Dog may have seemed unique until a few months after it opened, when it was joined, just blocks away, by a place called Japadog. Japadog served dogs with just Japanese toppings. Its signature was the Tcrimayo, with teriyaki sauce, Japanese mayonnaise, and seaweed. The spot began in 2005 as a cart run by a transplanted Japanese couple in Vancouver. By 2010, the couple had two carts. Then the Olympics came to town. The carts got famous, and the couple pursued their dream of opening a Japadog in New York.

The store debuted with a ceremony featuring two staffers dressed as ketchup and mustard bottles, with the labels "Ketchup" and "Mustard" crossed out. They symbolized confidence that New Yorkers would now be eating their hot dogs with miso sauce, wasabi mayonnaise, and bonito flakes. The menu included the Kurogoma Kimuchi, a turkey dog with kurogoma and kimchi; the Yakisoba, an Arabiki dog with Japanese noodles; the Gyoza Dog, a dog with gyoza, which is Japanese dumpling; and the Ume, a dog with sliced onion and plum sauce, which is ume sauce.

The dogs were hot for a while. But Japadog closed in 2014, leaving Asia Dog with the task of keeping a Western food Eastern. The stores weren't exactly rivals, but Asia Dog's survival still made it the winner. "People were impressed," Melanie says. "Now they ask us for advice."

BANTAM BAGELS

283 Bleecker St., New York, NY 10014

(646) 852-6320   bantambagels.com

READY TO ROLL

Bantams are a new food, and like any responsible new food they come with an instruction manual. Or anyway, an instruction note. "Bite The Hole," the note says at the top, to get your attention, which it does, since you usually think of a hole as the thing that does the biting. But the note explains. "How to Eat Your Bantam," it continues. "Our Bantams are best enjoyed when you bite the hole where they were filled. This keeps the filling inside the Bantam from your first bite to your last." That is, it keeps the filling from squirting onto your shirt.

A Bantam is a bagel, except that instead of a ring, it's a ball. The stuff that would be sandwiched into the ring is stuffed into the ball. The result is a miniature bagel that's more versatile than a full-size bagel, and that's often considerably neater to eat, as long as you bite the hole.

"We've definitely had a few cream-cheese incidents," says Nick Oleksak, who invented the Bantam. "One guy, on the first day, was sitting next to a display case, talking to his wife. He bit on the complete wrong side, and the cream cheese went onto the display case." It could have been worse. It could have gone onto his wife. In any case, people are gradually learning where to bite, and locating the hole is unquestionably a small price to pay in exchange for the chance to probe the big new world of the little loaded ball.

Bantams start with Basics: plain bagel, sesame-seed bagel, and everything bagel (the kind with multiple kinds of seeds, plus salt, garlic, and onion), stuffed with only plain cream cheese or butter. They're a first step for those who need proof that Bantams actually are bagels. The next step is Specials, of which there are about 15, chosen from a roster of about 30.

You could find combinations like these in big bagels, but you'd have to pick just one. With Bantams, you can pop maybe five or six. They're perfect for the indecisive.

Everybody's favorite is Everybody's Favorite, which is the everything bagel stuffed with vegetable cream cheese. But a close second is the French Toast, which is a cinnamon-nutmeg egg bagel with "a buttery, maple syr-upy cream cheese," though no bacon, yet. The Bleecker Street is a pizza-dough bagel filled with marinara-mozzarella cream cheese and topped with a slice of pepperoni. The Athena is a rosemary-oregano-basil bagel filled with olive-feta-spinach cream cheese and topped with a marinated tomato. There are monthly specials, like La Poquita, which is an Asiago-cheese bagel filled with chipotle chorizo cream cheese, and The Jack, which is a pumpkin-spiced bagel filled with sweet pumpkin cream cheese, with black sesame seeds on top. Happy Halloween.

You could reasonably ask how Nick dreamed all this up. The answer is that Nick dreamed all this up. One night in 2012, he says, he had a dream about little stuffed bagel balls. "I wrote it down on my iPhone. I'd never done that before. It was in the Notepad section."

He told his wife, Elyse, about the idea, and regardless of what she thought, she helped him start baking test bagels the next night. They opened the store in 2013. Elyse quit her Wall Street job; Nick kept his. He might be a dreamer, but he's a financially prudent dreamer.

There's been resistance. But just a little. There are New Yorkers for whom the bagel is something you simply don't turn into a little ball. "We had a cute little old lady come into the store with a friend," Nick says. "She said, 'Wait a minute, these aren't bagels!' Then she gave us the hand and stormed out."

BARBACON

836 Ninth Ave., New York, NY 10019

(646) 362-0622   barbacon.com

THE STRIP JOINT

Peter Sherman doesn't say that the red stripes on our flag represent strips of bacon, but he does say that strips of bacon represent America. It was on that premise that he chose to showcase America in New York by opening a restaurant at which all the food is made with bacon. The premise came to him when he was working with a Japanese chef whose brother had asked the chef to send him "something American." "What am I supposed to send him?" the chef asked Peter. Peter couldn't answer. But he also couldn't let go of the question.

"What is American?" he says. "It seemed like something I really should know. What signifies us? What represents us to other countries? Money?" He ruled out money. He ruled out a Coke. He ruled out hamburgers. ("They wouldn't travel well.") But it's surely a food, he concluded. And then he decided: bacon. Actually, he decided on smoked meats in general, but he went with the one that he felt was the most underappreciated. It's not clear whether the Japanese chef ever sent his brother some bacon. But it is clear that grappling with his question inspired Peter to conceive BarBacon.

"People had been doing barbecue artisanally for a while. But no one had caught on to the idea that we make bacon very, very well. People always throw bacon on things. But it deserved its own recognition. Why not make it the star? Why not make it the focus of the dish?" At BarBacon, that's what he's done. Or at the least he's made bacon the thing you look forward to, regardless of what else you order. You look forward to it on his grilled cheese. You look forward to it on his lobster roll. You look forward to it on his New England clam-and-corn chowder.

His menu starts with the basics, the first basic being the BLT, and the second basic being the BLT with fried egg and avocado. Next comes the BarBacon Burger. But then, if you're ready, the menu takes you to bacon that's been taken to places where it less frequently goes. There's the barbecued pork sandwich with bacon. There's the sausage, egg, and cheese sandwich with bacon. There's the bánh mì sandwich with Vietnamese-spiced soy-and-anise-glazed bacon. There's also the smoked-chicken club with bacon and the Caesar salad with bacon.

Peter makes no bones about bacon. "Bacon," his website says, "belongs to the hedonist, the throw-caution-to-the-winds sort who would eat a bacon sandwich with a side of bacon." That said, he also offers a four-bacon tasting, a four-bacon-and-four-beer flight, and assorted bacon-laced desserts.

Peter knows what he's doing, though he didn't intend to be doing it with bacon. He spent a decade cooking for chefs like Joël Robuchon and David Bouley. "It is the rarest of things to get where they got," he says. "Early on, I started thinking about how to separate myself."

Early on is when he met the Japanese chef, but when he was ready to create his own culinary art, he was still sure that his medium was bacon. He opened BarBacon in 2014. He liked the idea of a bar because, after all, you can get only so serious about bacon.

He was not the first in recent history to make a bacon splash. About a year earlier, Wesley Klein opened a bacon bakery called Baconery. It featured things like bacon cookies, bacon brownies, and chocolate-covered bacon, but it also had bacon sandwiches, all named after famous pigs. Baconery is still online, but the shop didn't last. BarBacon's in a better location, though—and it's a bar. "People are happy when they walk in here," Peter says. "It's fun. It's unpretentious. And you really can't screw up bacon. If it's overdone or underdone, it's still gonna be good."

BEYOND SUSHI

229 E. 14th St., New York, NY 10003

(646) 861-2889   beyondsushinyc.com

BEYOND THE SEA

Beyond" is a tricky concept. Take Bed Bath & Beyond. "Beyond" there can mean "kitchen," "backyard," "boot tray," or "Goobers." At Beyond Sushi, things are less complicated. "Beyond" there means "carrot," "avocado," and "mango," instead of "eel," "tuna," and "yellowtail."

This is no problem for sushi. The word, contrary to popular thought, does not refer to fish but rather to vinegar-flavored rice. But it can be a problem for customers who think that sushi does refer to fish and that, accordingly, "beyond" just means "really good fish."

At Beyond Sushi, though, there are no fish. There are fruits and vegetables. And rice, or else it would have to be Way Beyond Sushi. The restaurant slogan is "The Green Roll," and the restaurant logo has an H made out of two carrots and a kiwi slice. Not two eels and a blowfish. "Almost everybody says to us, 'How is it sushi without fish?'" says Tali Vaknin, who founded the restaurant with her husband, Guy Vaknin. She tells them how. At that point, however, she usually doesn't tell them how it's also a sushi place without being Japanese.

Yet it isn't. That "beyond" really has to work overtime. Though there are gobo and tofu and chopsticks, this is not a Japanese restaurant. But once you get beyond what Beyond Sushi is not and does not have, you're ready for the adventure of what it is and does have.

It has the Green Machine, made of six-grain rice, English cucumber, asparagus, and basil-marinated vegetables. It has the Mighty Mushroom, made of six-grain rice, enoki, tofu, shiitake, and micro arugula. It has the La Fiesta, made of black rice, avocado, chayote, pickled jalapeño, and cilantro. Those are among the eight rolls, each of which comes in eight pieces. There

are also six individual pieces. They are enoki, snow pea, carrot, mango, seaweed, and baked tofu, each comprising its namesake over six-grain or black rice. As you may have suspected, there is no white rice.

There is soy sauce. But it is not recommended. What is recommended is the sauce that each sushi comes with. The Green Machine comes with jalapeño wasabi. The Mighty Mushroom comes with shiitake teriyaki. The snow pea comes with carrot ginger; the carrot comes with toasted cayenne. The idea is not to irritate you, but to nourish you, Tali says. "We're a vegan restaurant. We're a healthy-lifestyle brand. We want to show people that eating a plant-based diet is not just healthy, but also tasty." And they want to do it, she adds, before fish disappear.

Guy Vaknin began his food career working with grains. He was a bartender. Still, he attended the Institute of Culinary Education. His employment prospects were good; his father owned a catering company. When he graduated, his father named him executive chef. Tali attended the Laboratory Institute of Merchandising and produced fashion shows, but she wanted to learn catering. Guy hired her in 2010. They were engaged in 2012 and married in 2013. By that time, they were also in business.

Guy wanted to get creative with fruits and vegetables, Tali says. He made vegan sushi and tried it out at corporate events. It went over well. He developed recipes with Bogi Tsoomonz, the sushi chef at the catering company. The restaurant opened in July 2012, and Guy has kept on creating. He makes a Roll of the Month and a Piece of the Month. One Piece of the Month was black rice with garlic-infused button mushrooms braised in a marsala wine sauce, topped with smoked paprika and micro chives with balsamic truffle porcini sauce.

It's showy. But showy educates, Tali says. And educate is what you must do when you are beyond. "We have a Spicy Mango roll," she says. "People say, 'This is a little like a spicy tuna roll.' I don't know where they get that, because there's no fish in it. But I'll take it."

Other locations: Chelsea Market, 75 Ninth Ave., New York, NY 10011, (212) 929-2889; 62 W. 56th St., New York, NY 10019, (646) 964-5097

THE BRUFFIN CAFÉ

Gansevoort Market, 52 Gansevoort St., New York, NY 10014
(844) 484-4100   thebruffin.com

STUFF IN MUFFINS

Sometimes you need to eat something that hasn't been invented, in which case it helps to know somebody who can invent it for you. Michael Bagley knew Medy Youcef, who cheerfully got to work when Michael said that he needed to eat a meal in the shape of a muffin. "I'm always on the run, and I wanted something different," Michael says. "I didn't want a sandwich, I didn't want a doughnut, I didn't want a piece of pizza. I wanted something that was totally self-contained, but not a sweet pastry. I told Medy, 'I have one free hand; see what you can do.'"

There were several things he could have done, considering that he and Michael were already running a bakery in upstate Orange County. What he did was to stuff brioche dough with cheddar cheese and bacon and bake it in muffin shape. It made a nice meal. It made a nice future.

"I named it the Bruffin," Michael says. "And then I wanted to see how versatile I could make it." So he turned to the world. It suggested creating international variations of the Bruffin. Eventually it suggested 16 of them. Eventually the men took them to New York. In 2013 they started selling them at the Smorgasburg market in Brooklyn. In 2014 they started selling them at two Bruffin Cafés. In 2015 they started shipping them across the country. We are, after all, more or less a nation with one free hand.

The world tour begins, of course, with the American Bruffin, with white Buffalo chicken, blue cheese, and hot sauce (that's the red part). It continues with the Canadian Bruffin, with maple Canadian bacon and cheddar, and the British and French, both with the pivotal bacon and cheese. The German Bruffin has frankfurter, sauerkraut, smoked Gouda, and horseradish mustard. The Swedish Bruffin has salmon, herbed goat cheese, capers, and

spinach. The Italian has pepperoni, pesto, and Parmesan; the Spanish has chorizo, Manchego cheese, and ancho chile.

Others range from the Greek, with spiced beef, feta, spinach, and kalamata olives, to the Indian, with masala curried chicken, chickpeas, and paneer. Each Bruffin is wrapped in colored paper and topped with a toothpick flag of its country. It supplies not only convenience but also brotherhood.

There are also sweet Bruffins, including the blueberry mascarpone cheesecake Bruffin and the chocolate-covered bacon and salted caramel Bruffin. But the Bruffin's major mission was to be a meal, which is what sets it apart from sundry other portmanteau pastries.

New York has been in a sort of hybrid hysteria, mostly aimed at a series of improbably mated baked goods. It was sparked in 2013 by the Cronut, the croissant-doughnut blend dispensed by Dominique Ansel at his eponymous bakery, if you got in line early enough.

Other options have included the Cr'nish (the croissant-knish), the Cretzel (the croissant-pretzel), and the Creffle (the crepe-waffle). But most have stayed purely pastries, whereas the Bruffin conjures up not only brioche, croissant, and muffin, but also meat pie.

"Unlike most pastries, the Bruffin is more savory than sweet," Michael says. "It's all about everything working together. The dough is rolled out flat, the ingredients are spread across the surface, and the dough is rolled up and cut. You get everything in every bite."

He is still creating. The cafe menu now also includes the Bruffin Bowl, which is a Bruffin stuck in a bowl of soup. But the principle is the same. "One of the keys to the success for the Bruffin," Michael says, "is that it's not just unique, but it's also perfectly proportioned."

CARACAS AREPA BAR

93½ E. Seventh St., New York, NY 10009

(212) 529-2314   caracasarepabar.com

CALL THEM INDESCRIBABLE

An arepa is a kind of bread that's used to make a sandwich that people tend to describe by invoking some other kind of sandwich. At Caracas Arepa Bar, they've heard descriptions like "Latin sloppy joe" and "pitalike pocket," not to mention "cake-swaddled mélange." Those might actually sound good to you. But Caracas strives for clarity. It defines arepas simply as "100% corn flour buns." They're among the buns with the good taste to stay in the background, allowing the spotlight to shine on the various medleys of food that are stuffed into them.

They are the bread of Venezuela, where they've been stuffed for hundreds of years, and where people are unlikely to call them "pitalike pockets." But it wasn't until 2003 that Caracas arrived in the East Village to raise their profile as one of the breads of New York.

It has succeeded. Not only is the original Caracas still a hot spot, but it has been joined by hot Caracases in Brooklyn and Queens. It offers traditional and untraditional fillings for the bread that, unfilled, has been described by invoking English muffins, corn muffins, and corn cakes.

Whatever it is, Caracas first grills it to make it crispy on the outside, and then bakes it to make it moist and steamy on the inside. And then it stuffs it and serves it with or without "Sidekicks." Without Sidekicks, you can probably handle two arepas, which will help you to discover your favorite stuff.

The traditional arepas begin with the bestseller, De Pabellón, which fills the bun with shredded beef, black beans, white salty cheese, and sweet plantains. Other classics include La Pelúa, with shredded beef and cheddar cheese, and Reina Pepiada, with chicken and avocado salad. At the opposite end of the tradition scale is Leek Jardinera, with grilled leeks, sun-dried

tomatoes, caramelized onions, and Guayanés cheese. Close behind is Playa Deluxe, tilapia with garlic-infused oil, sautéed mushrooms, avocado, pickled onions, and herb mayo.

Other possibilities range from De Pollo, with grilled chicken breast, caramelized onions, and cheddar cheese, to Los Muchachos, with grilled chorizo, spicy white cheese, jalapeños, and sautéed peppers. There's also the possibility of swapping the meats for baked tofu.

The Sidekicks include Guasacaca & Chips, which is guacamole; Tajadas, fried plantains with salty cheese; Yoyos, fried plantains with white cheese; Arroz con Caraotas, white rice and black beans; and Croquetas, deep-fried yucca-potato cakes with chorizo, corn, and cilantro.

All this can be yours thanks to the dot-com crash. Maribel Araujo came to New York just in time for it. She had a job with an Internet company, which she promptly lost. She had previously been a producer, and she ended up taking jobs as an independent-movie makeup artist. "One day we were shooting a movie in Brooklyn, and I went into a little tiny juice bar," Maribel says. "There was a guy there listening to Brazilian music, making juice, making sandwiches, and I said, 'Oh my God, this is exactly what I want. To work in a place like this, to talk to people.'"

She got what she wanted, with the help of Aristides "Gato" Barrios, who was then her husband and is still her business partner. They opened Caracas in 2003. In 2006 they took over a space two doors down. So now it's a split Caracas, with a Luke's Lobster in between. They've opened a bigger spot in Brooklyn, and a summer spot in Queens. And they keep doing their best to make clear what it is they sell. "There was a group walking out," Maribel says, "and I saw one talking to the other. She said, 'Oh my God, this is the best Mexican food I ever ate!'"

Other locations: 291 Grand St., Brooklyn, NY 11211, (718) 218-6050; 106-01 Shore Front Parkway, Queens, NY 11694, (718) 474-1709 (seasonal)

Also try: Palenque, Gansevoort Market, 52 Gansevoort St., New York, NY 10014, (718) 954-1955, palenquehomemadecolombianfood.com

CAVIAR RUSSE

538 Madison Ave., New York, NY 10022

(212) 980-5908   caviarrusse.com

THE ULTIMATE SPREAD

The first thing you might celebrate when you sit down at Caviar Russe is that you can afford to sit down at Caviar Russe. The next thing you might celebrate is that Caviar Russe has the ambiance of a restaurant that you would celebrate being able to afford. After that, you can celebrate whatever you want—birthday, wedding, graduation, nine-billion-dollar merger. And then you can celebrate being attended to the way you should at a place where you can spend 50 or more times what you'd spend at most places in this book.

In short, along with the roe, Caviar Russe offers refinement. It's the place where you get a taste of the elegant side of the city. You dine beneath Murano-glass chandeliers that look like champagne bubbles. You sit among fairy-tale murals. You have a fairy-tale time. "You're tucked away in a jewel-box setting; I don't think there's anything like it in the world," says David Magnotta, the owner of Caviar Russe. "The idea was to have a small, happy place where people could celebrate the milestones of their life, and we could celebrate our pride and joy—caviar."

Caviar is their pride and joy because it is their business. Caviar Russe is a caviar importer. It added the restaurant in 1997. The company supplies imported and domestic caviar to chefs across the country, and sells it online and at a caviar boutique inside the jewel box. David wanted a personal connection to caviar-lovers, so he set out to create "a caviar speakeasy for the twenty-first century." Here, he says, "you can completely immerse yourself in caviar. You might even come in because you want to teach your kids about caviar."

There are various means of immersion. You can have caviar by the spoon. You can have a caviar flight. You can have caviar service. You can have beggar's purses, which are crepes filled with caviar and crème fraîche. You can have a tasting, including courses with and without caviar. You can also have the full caviar-inspired tasting, which is seven courses (and at press time cost $395). "There's ten to fifteen grams of caviar in each course," David says. "By the time you're through, you've had three ounces of caviar."

Among the courses with built-in caviar are Peters Point Oyster, which has Meyer lemon, cucumber, classic Osetra, and borage; Diver Sea Scallop with classic Osetra (which is a crudo course); and Risotto, which has lobster, bone marrow, shiso, and Siberian caviar. Other courses include Blue Fin Tuna, with nori, sesame, radish, and ginger; Wild Striped Bass, with tomato, saffron, zucchini, and potato; Veal Loin, with asparagus, spring onion, and black garlic; and Morbier, with sweet pepper, basil, and sourdough.

The restaurant serves up to 10 caviars, which are among the ones on its website. At press time the site offered, for example, North American Shovelnose Sturgeon Caviar at $50 an ounce, and Caspian Sea Almas Osetra Caviar, at $595 an ounce.

If you get hooked on the caviar life, you can visit the boutique and equip yourself with mother-of-pearl caviar-serving accessories. They include large spoons, small spoons, mini spoons, sterling-tip spoons, oval plates, round plates, square plates, and a fork. But a visit to Caviar Russe need not involve immersion. You get in only as deep as you want to get. "We wanted this to be a place that enabled people to have a choice," David says. "You can just come in and have a glass of champagne and a spoon of caviar."

CRIF DOGS

113 St. Mark's Place, New York, NY 10009
(212) 614-2728   crifdogs.com

IT'S A MOUTHFUL

Brian Shebairo learned early that hot dogs have lives outside of New York, particularly since he grew up in New Jersey. They were, in fact, lives of debauchery, though at the time he didn't know it. When he did know it, he dutifully brought the debauchery over here. He brought the debauchery not only of the deep-fried hot dogs of his home state, but also of the similarly lurid hot dogs of other states. He brought dogs inspired by places like Rutt's Hut and Super Duper Weenie. In short, he brought New York City the hot dogs of America.

He discovered most of the dogs with Chris Antista, his partner in expeditions since their boyhoods in Hackensack. As kids, they found the local dog hot spots, of which, Brian says, "there was one every mile." As adults—sort of—they sought out the dogs of the Northeast.

They took weekly motorcycle rides. "We always ended up at a hot-dog place," Brian says. "It seemed like there wasn't any other food choice." It was a classic case of deprivation: "We kept leaving town to get hot dogs, because we couldn't get a good one here."

By "good," he didn't mean simply a tasty frankfurter. He meant a tasty frankfurter finished in something more arousing than sauerkraut. Their jaunts resulted in Crif Dogs, whose first name is the sound that Brian made one day when he tried to say "Chris" with a hot dog in his mouth.

At Crif, you can have sauerkraut free. Or you can have a Chihuahua. That's a deep-fried dog wrapped in bacon and covered with avocados and sour cream. If sour cream seems wrong, you can have a dog covered with cream cheese. Or a dog covered with cream cheese, scallions, and everything-bagel seeds.

To start your day, Crif Dogs offers a Good Morning, whose bacon-wrapped dog is covered with melted cheese and a fried egg. To start your day with a nod to your neighbor, there's Morning Jersey, whose cheese-and-egg-covered dog, instead of bacon, is wrapped in ham. For even more tastes of the Garden State, you can try the Garden State, a ham-wrapped hot dog with pepperoncini, American cheese, and mustard, or perhaps Jersey's Finest, still another ham-wrapped dog, this one covered with mustard, onions, and "our secret chili sauce." For a taste of the East, you might want to face the Tsunami, a bacon-wrapped dog with teriyaki sauce, pineapple, and green onions. For a taste of the South, you'd want to get your hands on a Spicy Redneck, a bacon-wrapped dog with chili, coleslaw, and jalapeños.

These and others are served in a suitably divey space, on a street whose late-night inhabitants are open to taking risks. The look fits the food, Brian says: "You don't want to feel like you're in a chemistry lab. You want to feel like you're in your mom's basement in high school."

Brian worked his way up to the basement starting when he was 12. He joined a pizza joint as a dishwasher and ended up making pies. Later on he was in construction while Chris was running a bar. But they were bound by hot dogs. They opened Crif in 2001.

Surprisingly, the business was not for Chris, and he left. But in 2009 Brian opened a second store, in Brooklyn. (In 2014 he opened one in the West Village, which quickly folded, perhaps because the previous tenant had sold hot dogs that were healthy.) "Crif Dogs," Brian explains, "is like a childhood memory. It's about your past. It's about a great day you had with your friends. You're coming here to have a hot dog. You're coming here to have fun. I'm a forty-one-year-old, two-hundred-thirty-six-pound little kid."

Other location: 555 Driggs Ave., Brooklyn, NY 11211, (718) 302-3200

BROOKLYN ONE-FOOD WONDERS

Brooklyn has a lot of things that Manhattan doesn't have. Among them is a store that sells nothing but mayonnaise. That alone is a good enough reason to include some of the wonders of Brooklyn, which will be waiting for you when you're ready to cross over the bridge.

Baba's Pierogies, 295 Third Ave., Brooklyn, NY 11215; (718) 222-0777; babasbk.com. Pierogies are plentiful in the East Village, but here you can get 'em in Gowanus.

Brooklyn Brine, 574A President St., Brooklyn, NY 11215; (347) 223-4345; brooklynbrine.com. The old pickle barrel never held Maple Bourbon Bread & Butter pickles, or pickled Moroccan Beans. The new jars here do.

Brooklyn Kolache Co., 520 DeKalb Ave., Brooklyn, NY 11205; (718) 398-1111; brooklynkolacheco.com. They stuff their kolaches with so many tasty things that you may not even care whether or not you know what a kolache is.

Brooklyn Porridge Co., 741 Union St., Brooklyn, NY 11215; (718) 623-6668; brooklynporridgeco.wordpress.com. Your porridge can have 42 toppings, but only from October to April. The rest of the year, this is an Uncle Louie G's.

Caracas Arepa Bar, 291 Grand St., Brooklyn, NY 11211; (718) 218-6050; caracasarepabar.com. Try some nontraditional fillings for the traditional bread of Venezuela, and read the story of Caracas Arepa Bar on page 18.

Clinton Hill Pickles, 431 DeKalb Ave., Brooklyn, NY 11205; (212) 334-3616. Get a taste of the old Lower East Side in a store that's descended from one of that neighborhood's most famous pickle places.

Crif Dogs, 555 Driggs Ave., Brooklyn, NY 11211; (718) 302-3200; crifdogs .com. This is where you go when you're ready to bite a dog that bites back. Read the story of Crif Dogs on page 24.

Doughnut Plant, 245 Flatbush Ave., Brooklyn, NY 11217; (212) 505-3700; doughnutplant.com. The square jelly doughnut now has a home here. Read the story of Doughnut Plant on page 33.

Dub Pies, 211 Prospect Park West, Brooklyn, NY 11215; (718) 788-2448; dubpies.com. They sell meat pies, of the kind you get in Australia and New Zealand, and they predate Tuck Shop and Pie Face in New York.

Empire Mayonnaise Co., 564 Vanderbilt Ave., Brooklyn, NY 11238; (718) 636-2069; empiremayo.com. Finally, mayonnaise in flavors like sriracha and lime-pickle. It does everything regular mayonnaise does, except with sriracha and lime-pickle.

Grand Central Oyster Bar & Restaurant Brooklyn, 256 Fifth Ave., Brooklyn, NY 11215; (347) 294-0596; oysterbarbrooklyn.com. It's not as grand or as central as the original at Grand Central, but it has the oysters—which are arguably more important than a vaulted ceiling. Read more on page 151.

Little Muenster Tiny Takeout, 145 Front St., Brooklyn, NY 11201; (646) 499-4331; littlemuenster.com. Here's a little chance to get a "super fancy" grilled cheese sandwich. Read the story of Little Muenster on page 51.

Luke's Lobster, 237 Fifth Ave., Brooklyn, NY 11215; (347) 457-6855; lukes lobster.com. Luke brings you a lobster roll (and a couple of other rolls) that won't break you. Read the story of Luke's Lobster on page 54. **Other location:** 11 Water St., Brooklyn, NY 11201; (917) 882-7516 (seasonal)

MatchaBar, 93 Wythe Ave., Brooklyn, NY 11249; (718) 599-0015; matcha barnyc.com. It may sound like a singles bar, but it's actually a green-tea-drink bar, which could actually make it a green-tea-drink-lovers' singles bar.

The Meatball Shop, 170 Bedford Ave., Brooklyn, NY 11249; (718) 551-0520; themeatballshop.com. Get your Daily Ball—not to mention an ice-cream sandwich—here. Read the story of The Meatball Shop on page 66.

Meltkraft, 442 Ninth St., Brooklyn, NY 11215; (347) 889-6290; meltkraft .com. If the grilled cheese with brisket and mac and cheese doesn't quite do it for you, have it grilled in duck fat. Read more on page 156.

O Live Brooklyn, 60 Broadway, Brooklyn, NY 11249; (718) 384-0304; olivebrooklyn.com. When you really care about olive oil, you come here and learn that Arbequina Melgarejo "boasts notes of creamy avocado and green almond." **Other location:** 140 Fifth Ave., Brooklyn, NY 11217; (718) 783-1680

Pelzer's Pretzels, 724 Sterling Place, Brooklyn, NY 11216; (347) 404-6720; pelzerspretzels.com. It takes courage to open a New York pretzel shop conceived on the premise that Philadelphia has better pretzels than New York.

The Pickle Guys, 1364 Coney Island Ave., Brooklyn, NY 11230; (718) 677-0639; pickleguys.com Brooklyn is a pickle paradise. Read more about The Pickle Guys on page 95.

Steve's Authentic Key Lime Pies, 185 Van Dyke St., Brooklyn, NY 11231; (718) 858-5333; stevesauthentic.com. It has just what the name says, and not much more. It's open to walk-ins on weekends, and sometimes on weekdays. Call first.

The Wheelhouse, 165 Wilson Ave., Brooklyn, NY 11237; (718) 483-9970; wheelhousebrooklyn.com. Build your own grilled-cheese sandwich, with your choice of 15 cheeses. It comes with a salad, to make you feel better.

CURRY-YA

214 E. 10th St., New York, NY 10003

(212) 995-2877   nycurry-ya.com

THE REAL JAPANESE FOOD

While you're nestled in a Japanese restaurant dining on California rolls and Philadelphia rolls and thinking that you're eating just like people in Japan, the people in Japan—allowing for the time difference—are most likely nestled in their homes gorging on plates of Japanese curry. It's curried sauce poured over rice, which to Americans may not sound like Japanese food, but to the Japanese is like American comfort food. It is said to be eaten regularly in typical Japanese homes. It is said to outrank even California rolls and Philadelphia rolls.

"Every household in Japan, north to south, cooks curry once a week," says Bon Yagi, who owns several Japanese restaurants, including Curry-Ya. "Each house makes it a little different," he adds. That would translate to roughly 47 million kinds of curry.

Bon has whittled that down to nine. But he makes the nine count. He bills Curry-Ya as the home of "Japanese gourmet curry." To explore that claim, you sit at a long white marble counter, choose your curry, and get your sauce delivered to you in a silver gravy boat.

The menu begins with Original Plain Curry, the restaurant's basic sauce, which is chicken and oxtail soup flavored with vegetables, fruits, and spices. Bon says that the restaurant cooks the bouillon for about six hours, though, considerately, it does that before you come in. There's the Vegetable Medley Curry, and the Japanese Classic, which has beef, potatoes, carrots, and pumpkin. There's the "Dry" Curry, with ground beef, chopped onions, carrots, celery, raisins, and hard-boiled egg, and the Hamburger Steak Curry, with a hamburger steak. There's also the Chicken Curry, with pan-fried chicken; the Chicken Katsu Curry, with a deep-fried chicken cutlet; the

Seafood Curry, with shrimp, squid, and scallops; and the Berkshire Pork Katsu Curry, with a deep-fried pork cutlet.

You can have any curry, except for the pork katsu and chicken katsu, baked with an egg and cheddar cheese on top. You can top anything with cheddar cheese, boiled egg, corn, natto, fried shrimp, vegetables, mini hamburgers, mini cutlets, or mashed-potato-and-ground-beef croquette.

There was probably no mashed-potato-and-ground-beef croquette on the menu when the Japanese discovered curry in the 19th century. Curry came to them from the British, who got the general idea from India. But since the Japanese got it from Britain, they considered it Western cuisine.

Still, they made it their own, which is why today's Japanese curry is something very different from Indian curry. Early on, they made curry with rice, which found its way into restaurants, though mostly upscale restaurants, even if back then no one called them upscale. It was in the 20th century that curry became a convenience food, beginning with the appearance of powdered instant curry. This was followed by block instant curry, then boil-bag curry, then microwavable curry, which is much easier to make than a California roll.

Bon Yagi didn't start with curry. His first New York restaurant was a 24-hour diner in the East Village. "But I thought to myself, I'm Japanese; I should have a Japanese-themed restaurant," he says. So he opened Hasaki, a classic spot that's over 30 years old. He's gone on to open places that showcase Japanese specialties from sake to noodles to octopus balls. He launched Curry-Ya in 2008, with the idea of restoring some elegance to a common dish: "This is more special. In Japan, curry is a part of everyone's life."

DOUGHNUT PLANT

379 Grand St., New York, NY 10002
(212) 505-3700   doughnutplant.com

SQUARING OFF

You deserve fruit in a fruit-named food. You deserve nuts in a nut-named food. You deserve evenly distributed jelly in a jelly-named food. In every case, Doughnut Plant gives you what you deserve—at least if the name of the food ends with "doughnut."

It may have been reasonable for people to think that doughnuts were perfect the way they were. But it was never reasonable for Mark Isreal. He was born to guide doughnuts to becoming greater than they were, and he did it six decades after New York got its first doughnut shop. He created fruit and nut doughnut glazes that were full of fruits and nuts. He created a square jelly doughnut whose jelly courses through every side. He created a crème brûlée doughnut with a blowtorched sugary shell. For each, he created unprecedented doughnut demand.

"First of all, I want Doughnut Plant doughnuts to be delicious," Mark says. "It just happens that they're made with high-quality ingredients. I also want to be original. I always thought that if I'm going to make doughnuts, I'm going to make the best doughnuts."

His fruit-glaze doughnuts include mango, banana, grapefruit, kiwi, grape, and pear. His nut-glaze doughnuts include peanut, macadamia, pistachio, walnut, cashew, and almond. You can complete those lists yourself, he says: "I don't think there's a fruit or nut I haven't tried." He has also tried seeds, like poppy, sesame, and sunflower, not to mention occasional leaves, flowers, and shrubs. He makes yeast doughnuts and cake doughnuts. Among the yeast favorites is Valrhona Chocolate. Among the cake favorites is Tres Leches, which is cake and milk in a doughnut.

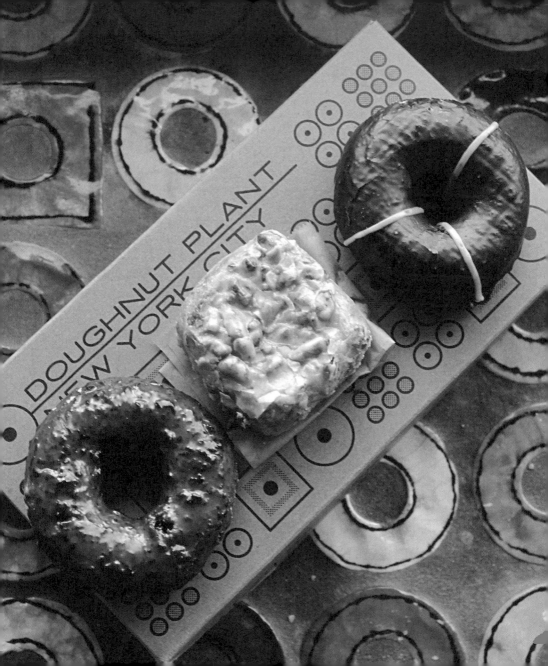

The square doughnuts have evolved to include fillings like Vanilla Bean & Strawberry Jam and Peanut Butter & Banana Cream. "You know how you eat the round doughnut with the big blob in the middle?" Mark says. "I didn't want to have a big blob in the middle."

That's the way you think when you have doughnuts in your background. A century ago, Mark's grandfather Herman Isreal worked in a bakery in St. Paul, Minnesota. He baked bread in the army and, in 1935, opened The College Pastry Shop in Greensboro, North Carolina. He began thinking up radical doughnut ideas. Mark's father, Marvin, glazed the doughnuts, but he moved on to other things. Mark came here in 1981 and also did other things—until he came upon Herman's doughnut recipes. Then he knew why he was here. He made doughnuts in his apartment, sold a dozen to his favorite coffee shop, and the coffee shop sold them all in two hours. He started making doughnuts every night, landed clients like Dean & Deluca, and delivered the doughnuts to them every morning on his mountain bike.

Cognizant that his roommate was living in a doughnut kitchen, he moved the kitchen to a basement and, in 2000, to his store. New York's first doughnut shop, Mayflower Doughnuts, opened in 1931. Doughnut Plant was arguably the biggest doughnut hit since. Mark followed his glazed doughnuts with his filled square doughnuts, his crème brûlée doughnut, and Doughseeds, his filled mini-doughnuts. He now has hundreds of doughnuts, including his Valentine's Day rose-petal doughnut and his Thanksgiving Day roasted-chestnut doughnut.

He has also opened two more Doughnut Plants, which brings up the name Doughnut Plant, which he explains: "My father used to work in a factory. In the morning my mother would say, 'Have a good day at the plant.' So the name was a way to include my mom in the business."

Other locations: 220 W. 23rd St., New York, NY 10011; 245 Flatbush Ave., Brooklyn, NY 11217

EGG SHOP

151 Elizabeth St., New York, NY 10012

(646) 666-0810   eggshopnyc.com

TAKE A CRACK AT IT

The answer, as it turns out, is "neither." The chicken and the egg came together. Or at least they do when you order the fully loaded egg salad sandwich at Egg Shop. Along with egg salad it has fried chicken. And if those two can come together now, they undoubtedly could have come together then.

Either way, the sandwich confirms the congeniality of the egg: If you can get along with your future self, you can get along with anything. That was loosely the premise on which Sarah Schneider based her little restaurant, which is based on sandwiches that are based on eggs.

Despite its name's implication, Egg Shop is not an egg joint. It's a joint at which everything is made with eggs. "The goal," Sarah says, "was to get people to think outside the box with eggs; to understand how versatile eggs could be for breakfast, lunch, and dinner." Thus, you don't want to come here thinking "Lumberjack Slam." You want to come here thinking "Grass Fed Tenderloin, Sunny Up, Chimi-Chili, Farm Greens, French Hero." Those are the components of the steak and egg sandwich, which is as close to conventional as the shop gets.

The bacon, egg, and cheese sandwich wears even more camouflage, even if it wears the name Eggshop B.E.C. It comprises "Broke Yolk, Shelburne Cheddar, Blackforest Bacon, Tomato Jam, Fresh Pickled Jalapeno, Panini Roll." Not even a mention of "egg" or "cheese." Other sandwiches include the Fish Out of Water ("Smoked Salmon, Pickled Egg, Fresh Dill, Caperberry Mustard, Rye") and The Beast ("Pulled Pork Carnitas, Sunny Up, Fresh Cilantro, Pickled Onion, Chipotle Bourbon Ketchup, French Hero"). Not for the lumberjack.

Besides the sandwiches there are eggy meals in bowls, called Cruisers, which include the Scrambler ("Soft Scramble or Whites, Scallion, Tomato, Seasonal Vegetables") and the Spandex ("Poached Egg, Miso Quinoa, Farm Greens, Avocado, Pickled Carrot"). And at night there are also Drunken Eggs, including Maple Sausage Sliders ("Fried Quail Egg, Housemade Sausage, Fresh Parsley, Vermont Maple Syrup") and Roe My Boat ("Salmon Roe, Potato Pancake, Sea Salt Yogurt, Cucumber, Pickled Onion, Fresh Dill").

It's not the coffee shop. But it wasn't meant to be the coffee shop. It was meant to be the coffee shop alternative for the egghead. "The idea came from not being able to find what I wanted in New York City, which is a rarity," Sarah says. "Usually everything is at my fingertips."

She discovered what she couldn't find when she left California for the Lower East Side, to become "a wild young party girl." "There's a New York City stereotype—young, broke, hung over in the morning. That was me," she says, charmingly with more pride than shame.

What she couldn't find was an unstereotypical egg sandwich. Since she couldn't find it, she found herself talking about it. She got someone to listen when she met Demetri Makoulis. She was working in denim—that is, she sold it—but she was soon working in eggs. She and Demetri (who's now her fiancé) hooked up with their chef, Nick Korbee, and their hospitality consultant, Florian Schutz. But the Egg Shop vision was Sarah's: "I had very specific ideas of what I wanted on the menu: things that were very healthy and things that were very indulgent."

When the shop opened, in 2014, she was gratified to find that the best-sellers were one of each: the Spandex and the B.E.C. She was even gratified, in a way, by the occasional complaints that she had no omelettes: "People have strong feelings about the egg," she says, "and what it means to them."

EMPIRE BISCUIT

198 Avenue A, New York, NY 10009
(646) 682-9529   empirebiscuit.com

OPEN TO ANYTHING

The biscuit with foie gras butter and preserved-lemon-and-cabbage jam has been ejected on the grounds of being over the top. The biscuit with roasted duck fat, thyme compound butter, and Cape-gooseberry-and-apricot jam has been retained on the grounds of being a classic. You might have made the same decisions. Then again, you might have no idea what any of that stuff tastes like, either alone or together. In any case, you might like knowing that at the top of Empire Biscuit is a chef who is using a comfort food to nudge you out of your comfort zone.

After all, adventure is what places like this are about, and there isn't too much adventure in a Pillsbury Grands with grape jelly. There's much more in a fresh-baked biscuit with Gorgonzola-and-nutmeg butter and candied-mango jam, which Empire suggests as a first step.

For the intransigent, there is plenty of old-fashioned comfort. Empire's top sellers, in fact, are its biscuit with sausage and gravy; its biscuit with bacon, egg, and cheddar; and its biscuit with spiced fried chicken, even if it does have pickled carrots and sauce à l'orange. But the chef, Jonathan Price, sees his biscuit house as a laboratory for compound butters, cheeses, spreads, jams, jellies, and marmalades. For him the buttery biscuit is a backdrop for combos like The Lemony Susan, with brown butter and lemon curd, and The Vacación, with spiced-rum butter and banana pudding.

Among other choices on the combo rotation are Your Mother's House, with maple-syrup butter and pumpkin-pie spread; The You Oughta Know, with pimento cheese and red-pepper jelly; and The Snuggah Boo, with plum, prune, and port jam, and goat-cheese-and-black-pepper butter. But you're also free to be your own chef and choose any two things from the

latest list of seductively challenging toppings. Besides the ones mentioned, they could include arugula-and-fennel butter, sweet-onion jam, and grilled-pineapple, dried-cherry, and jalapeño jam.

These are not toppings you will find in Southern biscuit chains like Biscuitville, whose menu includes the Bologna Biscuit and the Liver Mush

Biscuit. That doesn't mean that New Yorkers wouldn't like those two. It just means that Jonathan wanted to create a biscuitville of his own.

He began by being born in Virginia and growing up in Florida. He took a detour by taking the LSATs and applying to law schools. But while he applied, he took a job in a French bistro in Florida. "Something about working in a restaurant just clicked for me," he says. Instead of becoming a law student, he became head waiter at Magnolia Grill in North Carolina. (His Ben and Karen combo is named after its chefs.) When he moved to New York, he became captain at Bouley. That's where he met a waiter and fellow Southerner named Yonadav Tsuna.

They would become partners, but at first they became friends, while Jonathan toyed with ideas that were wrong. One was for an underground event space where a different chef would cook every night. One was for a fried-fish joint that would serve biscuits and gravy late. He threw back the fish because of expense, but he stuck with the biscuits. He and Yonadav got to work on the biscuit place. They named it Empire after its state and gave it the look of a "modernist farmhouse." In late 2013 it opened. The day after it opened, it closed.

Demand exceeded supply. But when they matched, Jonathan got proud. "My personal favorite is butter and clementine marmalade," he says. "When I eat that, I feel good about what we're doing here. When I'm down, I eat one of those and I think, 'We're not so bad. We're OK. This is good.'"

FLEX MUSSELS

174 E. 82nd St., New York, NY 10028

(212) 717-7772   flexmussels.com

COMING ON STRONG

Bobby and Laura Shapiro brought back a nice souvenir of their vacation: a mussel restaurant. They must have had a really big car. They wanted you to taste what inspired them to bring back the souvenir, which is also what inspired them to buy a house in the place where they had the vacation. The place is Prince Edward Island, one of the Canadian Maritimes, and the one whose nickname, PEI, often precedes the word "mussels." As for Prince Edward, he was the first prince to enter the United States. He walked here from Canada, thus blazing the trail for the Shapiros' restaurant.

The restaurant has made a star as well as a pun of the mussel, the bivalve mollusk that rarely gets a home of its own. Of course, it was in oyster beds that New York City gastronomy was conceived. But besides oyster bars, we've had clam bars and lobster bars. Flex Mussels stepped in to be the domicile of mussels. Its menu offers mussels served about two dozen ways. The offerings get as simple as the Classic, which is mussels with white wine, herbs, and garlic. But they're collectively an invitation to travel the world.

For a trip to India, you get the Bombay, which is mussels with Indian curry, garlic, cinnamon, star anise, and white wine. For a trip to Thailand, you take the Thai—the bestseller—which is mussels with curry coconut broth, lemongrass, kaffir lime leaf, coriander, lime, ginger, and garlic. If Mexico's your destination, the Mexican takes you there with mussels in chipotle adobo, chorizo, calamari, and posoles. If you prefer Denmark, the Copenhagen gives you mussels with Danish blue cheese, double-smoked bacon, spinach, and cream, though no Danish. For the tastes of Italy, there's a San Daniele, a Parma, and a Fra Diavolo, not to mention an Italiano. And if you

like to be closer to home, there's the Maine, with lobster, smoked bacon, and chowder, and the Southern, with Dijon mustard, ham, corn, and bourbon.

The choices total 22, but there's a No. 23, reserved for an unusual mussel dish, in case you see the others as usual. No. 23s have included the Idaho—mussels with baked potato, cheddar cheese, and bacon—and the Triple M, for mussels, meatballs, and marinara.

Bobby and Laura Shapiro were almost certainly not envisioning mussels with meatballs when they first visited PEI about 20 years ago. But they loved the island. "We went back ten years later to see if it was still as wonderful as we remembered, and it was," Laura says.

Bobby had been opening restaurants in New York for years, so the couple opened one on PEI. Then they got a house there. Their restaurant was Dayboat; Flex Mussels was a nearby shack. But they took it over, and later, with their daughter, Alexandra, they brought it to the Upper East Side as a restaurant. That was in 2008—just in time for the recession. But Flex Mussels turned out to be just the thing for the recession. "It was a hit from the moment we opened the door," Laura says. "We were at the right price, in the right neighborhood, with the right concept."

In 2010 the family opened their second Flex, in the West Village. Both restaurants are decorated with photos and paintings of PEI. And both restaurants have a Not Mussels menu, for people who don't care to travel. Appropriately, the Not Mussels menu includes a selection of oysters.

Both restaurants also have Flex Donuts, whose name doesn't work as well, but names don't really matter with doughnuts. As for the restaurant's name, the Shapiros didn't coin it, but Laura says they love it—"although we do get a lot of calls asking about massages and what time our gym opens."

Other location: 154 W. 13th St., New York, NY 10011, (212) 229-0222

THE KATI ROLL COMPANY

99 MacDougal St., New York, NY 10012
(212) 420-6517   thekatirollcompany.com

MEAL WITH A PEEL

The Kati Roll Company so wants you to love kati rolls that it not only sells them, but also teaches you how to eat them. "Hold roll firmly," begins the illustrated tutorial on its website. "Find top edge of paper. Tear a little to expose roll. Take bites. Keep tearing paper around roll. Take more bites." From there you're on your own, though you can always return to "Hold roll firmly."

Mastering proper technique can only enhance your enjoyment, says Payal Saha, the founder of The Kati Roll Company. "We would go to the store and see people do horrible things," she explains. "They would unwrap the whole thing at once and it would all fall apart." That just won't do with a kati roll, since its attraction lies in its meticulous blending of meats, vegetables, spices, and textures. And it's especially important to Payal that you enjoy your kati roll, because it's most likely because of her that you've gotten a kati roll.

A kati roll, also known as a kathi roll or a kati kebab (or a kathi kebab), is a street food from Calcutta, also known as Kolkata. Nizam's, a Calcutta restaurant, claims that its founder was the roll's inventor, which is why the kati, or kathi, roll is also known as a Nizami roll. It's said to have been invented in the early 1900s, when the inventor sold it from a cart to fussy Englishmen. Indulging their fussiness, he started wrapping the roll in paper. That led to success, which led to the restaurant and, a century later, to The Kati Roll Company.

There, your kati roll begins with your choice of bread—the traditional paratha, which is white and fried on the grill, or the roti, which is whole wheat and grilled without oil. But after that, you have just one more step: You pick your roll. You have no obligation to design it.

The bestseller is the Chicken Tikka Roll, made with marinated chicken cooked on a skewer. (One definition of *kati* is "skewer.") Next is the Achari Paneer, made with farmer cheese (paneer), pickling spices (achar), and grilled peppers and tomatoes. It's the vegetarian's choice.

There's the Unda Roll, with omelette-style egg; the Aloo Masala Roll, with fried potatoes; the Unda Aloo Roll, with egg and potatoes; the Unda

Chicken Roll, with chicken and egg; the Unda Beef Roll, with beef and egg; and the Beef Tikka Roll, with no chicken, no potatoes, and no egg.

Rolls like these have been on New York menus before, but Payal set out to give them a New York home of their own. She did this when she determined that her degree in sociology from the University of Delhi wasn't going to put kati rolls on her table. "I didn't learn very much in college," she says. "I graduated because it was not acceptable for me not to graduate." She spent some time working in film but knew that her passion was in food—especially the food that she got from carts when she was growing up in Calcutta.

She meant to introduce it near Wall Street, but fate led her to MacDougal. She opened The Kati Roll Company there in 2002. The store posted the words "Fast! Tasty!! Portable!!!" New Yorkers liked that. Soon the place needed a bouncer from midnight to five. "I opened the store with my cleaning lady," Payal recalls. "We opened the door and started selling food." She thought the novelty would wear off soon. It didn't. "When I made a thousand dollars on a Saturday night, I called my father in Calcutta. I couldn't believe my luck."

Now she has three stores in New York and one in London. An attempt at a fancier place, called Babu, kept her grounded in street food. "I didn't dream this," she says. "I didn't think it would do that well. I opened with my cleaning lady. I have sixty-five people now."

Other locations: 49 W. 39th St., New York, NY 10018, (212) 730-4280; 229 E. 53rd St., New York, NY 10022, (212) 888-1700

LA MAISON DU CROQUE MONSIEUR

17 E. 13th St., New York, NY 10003
(212) 675-2227 croquemr.com

THE SANDWICH LOVERS

Y ou can be reasonably sure that your restaurant will be unique if you dedicate its menu to the French toasted ham-and-cheese sandwich called a croque-monsieur, but you can be extra-sure that it will be unique if you dedicate its design to the French erotic writer and literary lover Anaïs Nin.

The writer has no historical connection to the sandwich, but the creation of the restaurant brought the two together. And it's a perfect match, says Alberto Benenati, one of the creators: *Croque-monsieur* means "crunch man," which, at least in a sense, he says, is what Nin did.

Alberto and his partner, Yves Jadot, have been serving the croque-monsieur for years at Petite Abeille, their chainlet of Belgian comfort-food restaurants. They were shown the space on E. 13th Street and deemed it too small even for a restaurant named Petite. But not too small for one sandwich.

After taking the two-story house, they first discovered that it was built in 1910—possibly the year of birth of the croque-monsieur. They then discovered that it was the house that Nin rented in 1944, to run a press to print her works. Her rent was $65 a month.

The owners made Nin their muse and restored the space to evoke the look of an old-time print shop, complete with wooden printers' drawers. Then they fused their parallel themes by naming each one of their sandwiches Mister followed by the first name of one of Nin's men.

Thus the menu begins with Mr. Henry, named for Henry Miller. It's the classic croque: ham with a choice of cheese and a dollop of béchamel. Next comes the one exception: Mme. Anais, which has the same ingredients plus an egg. It's what's known as the croque-madame. Among the New Croques are Mr. Antonin, which has turkey, provolone, and cranberry sauce; Mr. Lawrence, which has spicy tuna and cheddar; Mr. Eduardo, which has bresaola, smoked mozzarella, and béchamel; and Mr. James, which has smoked salmon and herbed goat cheese. There are vegetarian croques, including Mr. Gore (Vidal), which has portobello mushrooms, sun-dried tomatoes, pine nuts, and goat cheese. And there are sweet croques, like Mr. Gonzalo (Moré), which has banana, Nutella, and mascarpone. Gonzalo was the mister who helped run the printing press.

The Nin theme runs through the two floors, in portraits of the author and her men, accompanied by short biographies of the men. Nor are the stairs overlooked; some of the steps bear quotations from the author, like "Good things happen to those who hustle."

That would seem to apply to the owners, who undoubtedly have to hustle to run several successful restaurants in New York. Yves founded Petite Abeille in 1995. Alberto joined him a few years later. Now they have four Abeilles and the Croque, which opened in 2012.

With Jason Hicks, the Croque chef, they also have the British spots Jones Wood Foundry, the Peacock, and the Shakespeare; the cocktail spot Raines Law Room; and the Mexican spot ¡Vamos! As Nin says on another step, "Dreams are necessary to life." As for the croque, it may have been invented in a Parisian cafe. Or it may have been invented in a lunch box. The popular story holds that it was just a ham-and-cheese sandwich until a French worker left his lunch box on a radiator and the sandwich attained croquehood.

Regardless, it's made a round-trip: In 2014 La Maison du Croque Monsieur opened a branch in Paris. "I think they were surprised," Alberto says of Parisians. "Maybe not stunned, but surprised. I think their reaction was, 'How did we not think about doing this?'"

LITTLE MUENSTER

Hudson Eats at Brookfield Place, 225 Liberty St., New York, NY 10281
(212) 786-0186   littlemuenster.com

THE CHEESE LOVERS

Vanessa Palazio and Adam Schneider make a nice grilled-cheese sandwich. Coincidentally, they also make a nice couple. Being a nice couple, of course, only helps the sandwiches, just as being nice sandwiches only helps the couple. This symbiotic cycle seems to be a matter of destiny, since cheese has been binding this pair from the start. "We've thought about how quickly we went from dating to talking about doing this business together," Vanessa says. "But it just all made sense."

Little Muenster is not the city's first grilled-cheese-sandwich restaurant, but then, the first ones didn't last. This one has several years under its belt, which is most likely because of its nice sandwiches and its nice couple, not to mention its cheese-grater chandelier. It serves what it bills as "super fancy" grilled-cheese sandwiches, which, for most of us, are ones with cheese fancier than Velveeta. But its sandwiches are surprising, unless your home version of grilled cheese is, say, Gruyère and Muenster with leek confit, chevre, and crispy pancetta.

That's one of the favorite selections. Another is the Butternut Squash, which, besides butternut squash, has Muenster, Asiago, Parmesan, and sage brown butter. Another is the French Onion, made with Muenster, Gruyère, fresh arugula, and caramelized onions. For something meatier, there's the Cuban, with slow-roasted pork and Virginia ham, along with Muenster, Swiss, pickles, and smoky chipotle mayo. And for something else, come back some other month, since the menu "rotates and changes with the seasons."

The sandwiches are undeniably fancy, and yet you can make them fancier with extras from tomato to avocado mash. Or you can strip them down

to Muenster and white American or cheddar. That's called The Classic. And if it's your choice, you're not alone. It's the number-one seller.

This suggests that Vanessa and Adam could have done all right selling just Classics with maybe a Coke and a side of chips. But they dreamed higher. Adam, in fact, dreamed of being an astronaut. Vanessa dreamed of being a steak-house owner. Either way, it was higher.

Vanessa had the cheese background. Her parents owned two supermarkets, and she worked in the cheese department of the one in Brooklyn Heights. "I always had the Key Food brand of Muenster cheese, and it was delicious," she says. It became half of her future restaurant's name. Her grandfather was the one who got her parents into supermarkets, and also the one who got her into steak houses. He took her to Peter Luger, to Smith & Wollensky, to The Palm. She wanted one of her own. She became a paralegal, but then she studied hospitality at NYU.

While in college, she met Adam. He wasn't an astronaut; he was a food photographer. But he already had his hand in cheese. For their third date, he invited her to a macaroni-and-cheese contest. He was in it. He lost. But he won her interest, if not her vote. They started talking cheese, and though their tastes were different, they fell in love with the idea of a grilled-cheese restaurant. "We bought a lot of bread, we bought a lot of cheese, and we started making food for each other," Vanessa says. Yes, the story gets gooey.

They enlisted a chef, who stuffed them with sandwiches till they had to throw parties so that he would instead stuff their friends with sandwiches. They opened Little Muenster on Stanton Street in 2011. "Little" was Vanessa's nickname for her dog.

In 2012 the couple opened a store in Brooklyn; in 2014 they moved their Manhattan store to Brookfield Place. In between, they got married. But not with a cheese theme, Vanessa says: "My mother said, 'This isn't a restaurant opening. This is your wedding.'"

Other location: 145 Front St., Brooklyn, NY 11201, (646) 499-4331

LUKE'S LOBSTER

93 E. Seventh St., New York, NY 10009

(212) 387-8487   lukeslobster.com

CRUSTACEAN BREAK

There's a convention that enables restaurants to put lobster on a bun and sell it for about $30. You could call this the lobster roll. Luke Holden questioned the convention. Now he puts lobster on a bun and sells it to you for a lot less. And yet his lobster rocks. In other words, at Luke's, you get a reasonably sized roll at a reasonable price, plus a pittance more for chips, a pickle, and pop. It was a deal whose time had come, and it's a deal whose time keeps coming: Luke already has several locations, and he's on his way to more.

Yes, lobster is costly. But it doesn't have to break you. Luke knew this because he grew up in a lobster family in the lobster state. Though they had earned their esteem as a delicacy, lobster rolls had become too lofty. Luke made it his business to bring them down to earth. He also made it his business to keep them delicacies, especially since the 30-dollar rolls sometimes are not. His rolls would have the best Maine lobster, and it would not be drowning in goo. And the rolls would be as affordable as any number of New York burgers.

The menu clarifies their simplicity: "The seafood is served chilled atop a buttered and toasted New England–style, split-top bun with a swipe of mayo, a sprinkle of lemon butter and a dash of our secret spices." If you love lobster, you gotta love swipes, sprinkles, and dashes.

The lobster roll is Luke's bread and butter, but there are a couple of crustaceous alternatives. They are the crab roll and the shrimp roll. And if you think they're just cheaper alternatives, keep in mind that Luke's favorite is the shrimp roll, and he gets the employee discount. If you can't decide, Luke's offers the Taste of Maine, which gives you some of practically

everything on the menu. You get half a lobster roll, half a crab roll, half a shrimp roll, two Empress crab claws, chips, a pickle, and pop, at a popular price.

All this opportunity began in a small town in Maine named Cape Elizabeth, where Luke's father, Jeff, ran a seafood plant. As a boy, Luke worked on the docks. As an older boy, he built a skiff and fished for lobster with his brother Mikey. It's still the job he misses the most. He went to Georgetown University and learned finance and management, which was good for his future but not for his soul. He got a job as an investment banker and held on to it while he hatched his plan to open a lobster shack in the East Village. He was saving up for the pay cut.

That is just what he took when he left the bank job. Fortunately, his shack was a hit from its opening, in 2009. He opened it with a partner, Ben Coniff, whom he located on Craigslist. The following year the Upper East Side and the Upper West Side got shacks of their own. Those are actually more like restaurants; at the original you can imagine you're right on the beach if you don't look at the hardware store across the street. That first one is now the smallest but, in Luke's words, it's "the heart and soul." After all, one wall has a 3D boardwalk.

Luke now runs a seafood company along with restaurants not only in New York, but also in Washington, DC. Yet his heart remains on that hand-made boat back in Cape Elizabeth. "I wish I was out there catching the lob-sters," he says. "That's my ultimate goal—to return to that one day."

Other locations: 26 S. William St., New York, NY 10004, (212) 747-1700; 207 E. 43rd St., New York, NY 10017, (646) 657-0066; The Plaza Food Hall, 1 W. 59th St., New York, NY 10019, (646) 755-3227; 426 Amsterdam Ave., New York, NY 10024, (212) 877-8800; 242 E. 81st St., New York, NY 10028, (212) 249-4241; 11 Water St., Brooklyn, NY 11201, (917) 882-7516 (seasonal); 237 Fifth Ave., Brooklyn, NY 11215, (347) 457-6855

LUMPIA SHACK SNACKBAR

50 Greenwich Ave., New York, NY 10011

(917) 475-1621   lumpia-shack.com

SPRINGTIME FOR MANILA

You know your Chinese thing. You know your Japanese thing. You may also know your Indian thing, your Vietnamese thing, and your Thai thing. But chances are, you don't know your Filipino thing. Getting you to know that thing is Lumpia Shack Snackbar's thing. The restaurant feeds you the flavors of the Philippines, with a fixation on figuring out your Filipino favorites. It showcases these flavors in finger-size snacks called lumpia, which are essentially spring rolls, which may sound Chinese but are Chinese only to a point.

"Thai restaurants, Chinese restaurants, Japanese restaurants—they all have dishes adapted to the Western palate," says Neil Syham, the lumpia chef. "That's what we're trying to do in our restaurant. I was born in the Philippines and raised in the States. I know the Western palate." He knows that the Western palate—or at least the New York City palate—likes foods that are tasty, so he offers that. He also knows that the Western palate likes food to be crunchy, so he offers that. His lumpia are Shanghai-style, meaning that they are deep-fried.

On occasion, he offers the fresh-style lumpia more customary in the Philippines as daily specials. But mostly he offers crunchy. He wants his customers to come back. "Most people, we find, enjoy fried food more than the healthy alternatives. We get a great reaction to it." The rolls' big crunch and small size can entice Filipino-food novices to take a chance on things that might seem less enticing in the open. These include things like Sisig, which here comprises pork belly, ears, and jowls, and Lechon Paksiw, which is roast pork with liver sauce.

Among other lumpia are Original Pork, Peking Duck, Sinigang Shrimp, Chicken Adobo, and Truffled Adobo Mushroom, along with Kare-Kare, which is oxtail; Bicol Express, which is pork and coconut milk; Pinakbet, which is okra, squash, and bitter melon; and Bulalo, which is beef and bone marrow. For a bigger taste of the Philippines, there are also some soups, sandwiches, and rice bowls. Among the rice bowls is the Fried Bangus, which is boneless marinated milkfish with spiced vinegar, brown rice, herb salad, and pickled radish, topped with fried garlic and fried shallots, for crunch.

You get this chance to discover which Filipino food is right for you because Neil got the chance to discover which career was wrong for him. That one was advertising, which he got into in 2002 and which ensured that he'd soon be working at a stove instead of a desk. He went to culinary school, became a chef, and married Angie Roca, who was born in the Philippines and raised in Canada. She was a nurse, but together they were a Filipino-food team. By 2012, they were at Smorgasburg in Brooklyn selling Neil's specialties.

The specialties were a hit, which Neil allows may have had to do with his Western-palate adapting. "Our food is more Filipino-inspired," he says. "We show the flavors of the Philippines in a different way. And we were lucky that people enjoyed the food and the flavors." He had yet to make Filipino the new Chinese, but in the meantime he opened the Lumpia Shack Snackbar in 2014. And he keeps trying, with creations like his version of the dessert halo-halo—which, while it's pronounced "hollow hollow" turns out to be anything but.

It's shaved ice with coconut, bananas, berries, palm seeds, coconut jelly, leche flan, milk foam, purple yam purée, purple yam whipped cream, and kettle corn. It looks like fireworks. And yet it's not traditional. For the Western palate, Neil left out the boiled kidney beans. And the garbanzos.

MARCHI'S RESTAURANT

251 E. 31st St., New York, NY 10016

(212) 679-2494   marchirestaurant.com

TAKE WHAT YOU GET

Most places in this book spotlight one food in many combinations. Marchi's spotlights many foods in one combination. It gives you no ordering options. It gives you no building steps. It gives you no responsibility, because it gives you no menu. It gives you food, in five courses. The same food and the same courses. Six nights a week. As it's been doing for the past 70 years.

Marchi's is the secret dining club that will let you in. It's also the place to have dinner when you don't want to make decisions. You come in, you sit down, you get served. You eat for an hour or two. You get a feeling that's vaguely familiar. Then you remember: You're relaxed.

Marchi's is secret because, through the years, it's been somewhat forgotten, maybe because it has no sign and it doesn't advertise. But if you find it, and you're not set on an edgy night out, it will give you a meal that you'll surely enjoy and probably never forget.

The meal begins with warm bread but no butter, lest you spoil your appetite. Forget the butter. Focus instead on the sprawling antipasto. It includes red-cabbage tuna salad, Genoa salami, honeydew melon, radishes, celery, tomatoes, and fennel. All artistically arranged. Your second course is lasagna. Specifically, Lorenzo Lasagna, just as the red-cabbage tuna salad was Lorenzo Salad. Both are named for Lorenzo Marchi, the founder of the feast and the creator of lasagna and tuna you never dreamed of, especially at the same meal.

After the lasagna you get fried fish, which comes with green beans and beets. After that you get roast chicken and veal, with tossed salad and sautéed mushrooms. After that you get fresh fruit, provolone, warm lemon

fritters, and crispy crostoli, along with the sense that you've been cared for by Grandma and Grandpa, which you have.

They are the late Lorenzo and Francesca Marchi, and when you dine at Marchi's, you're dining in what was once their house. It's where, in 1929, Francesca was cooking meals created by Lorenzo—the aromas of which tormented Louis DeMarco.

Louis was the bachelor who lived in the apartment above and who finally came downstairs to ask if he could come in and eat. He offered the Marchis 50 cents. Times being what they were, they accepted. Louis not only kept coming, but started bringing his friends. Before long, the Marchis' home was an apartment that was a restaurant. They always served one meal a night, but at first they changed the meal nightly. During the Second World War, they stuck with one lineup. After the war, they went back to changing—but the patrons now rejected change.

"The customers said, 'Go back to what you were doing,'" says Mario Marchi, the son of Lorenzo and Francesca. So the family refined what they were doing into a showpiece Northern Italian dinner, and that's what they've been serving since. It's something in life you can count on.

It was also enough to make Marchi's a hot spot. In midcentury, it actually did provide an edgy night out. It attracted guests like Marilyn Monroe, Grace Kelly, and Sophia Loren, and when you had dinner with people like that, you didn't worry about a menu.

Marchi's is still run by Mario with his wife, Christine, and his brothers, John and Robert. And it still feels like home, with its curtains, carpeting, fireplace, and vintage paintings. But it's become a bigger home, now with five dining rooms, along with an outdoor dining garden. And yet, Mario says, it's getting tougher to get people in, because it's getting tougher to get people to take their time. On top of that, he adds, there are people who just seem to need their choices. Even after he's served them five courses, some patrons will say things like: "What? You don't have ice cream?"

MEATBALL OBSESSION

510 Sixth Ave., New York, NY 10011

(212) 260-8646   meatballobsession.com

YOUR CUP RUNNETH OVER

Daniel Mancini rushed home from school for lunch because he knew what lunch would be: his grandma's meatballs with sauce, cheese, and bread, in a coffee cup. Years later, he wanted to share that pleasure, improved by leaving out school. That's why he built the Home of the Original Meatball in a Cup.

It's not Grandma's home, and it's not Grandma's cup, but it is Grandma's meatball. It's served as it was served to Daniel, except in a paper cup. And the Home is a testament to Daniel's obsession with that meatball, which is why its name is actually Meatball Obsession.

It's a window behind which are, along with a person, pots whose primary colors indicate the kind of meatballs they contain. The red holds beef (Grandma's original); the yellow, turkey; the blue, pork sausage. Your meatball comes with sauce, Parmesan dipping bread, and your choice of cheese.

To keep to tradition you choose Original, which is Parmigiano-Reggiano, Locatelli Pecorino Romano, or mozzarella cheese pearls. To step out on Grandma, you choose Regional, which is Bari (smoked scamorza and hot peppers) or Genoa (toasted pine nuts, olive oil, and Pecorino Romano). Recent topping additions include gnocchi, mini-ravioli, and Dan's Savory Toppings, which are sautéed peas and onions; roasted cauliflower; sautéed red peppers, onions, and baby bella mushrooms; and a combination of five cheeses with olive oil, which sounds rich even for Grandma. Originally, you could also choose between a cup and a pocket. Not your pants pocket— a ciabatta-bread pocket. But the pocket is on its way out because most people prefer the cup. This confirms Daniel's belief that people like tradition more than they think.

HOME OF THE ORIGINAL MEATBALL IN A CUP

OPEN

A

Daniel grew up in Brooklyn, conveniently in the same house as Grandma, who was also known as Anna Mancini. He ran home for lunch on Mondays because that was the day when she had meatballs left over from the family meatball dinners that she cooked on Sundays. In spite of his passion, he had a career in clothes, starting as a clerk in bygone department stores and rising to president of a clothes company. But he never forgot the meatballs. And when he decided that he'd sold enough clothes, he switched to meatballs, though first in stores rather than in cups.

In 2007 he launched MamaMancini's, which now, he says, puts Anna's meatballs in 9,000 supermarkets. That might seem like success, except that his dream from the start was to sell the meatballs straight from the pot. MamaMancini's was a vehicle for product promotion. With the meatballs promoted, he opened Meatball Obsession in 2012. It had been predated by The Meatball Shop, but then, that had been predated by his meatballs. "I claim credit for the explosion in meatballs," he says. "MamaMancini's did put the meatball out there."

It's a good meatball. The original is ground beef with bread crumbs, Pecorino Romano, eggs, onion, parsley, salt, and pepper. Meatballs are one of those things like chocolate-chip cookies or pancakes: It's not so hard to make a good one, and yet there are so many bad ones.

Dan tried a chicken meatball, but he let the turkeys keep their job. And he has resisted the mild pressure to serve a vegetarian meatball. "People do occasionally ask for it," he says. "But it's an oxymoron. I tell them, 'The sign says *Meat*ball Obsession.'"

Still, he wants his customers happy. Before he opened the store, he wondered whether people would want their meatballs in a cup. So far they do. "The best thing about Meatball Obsession," he says, "is you hand someone the cup, and they just smile."

THE MEATBALL SHOP

84 Stanton St., New York, NY 10002

(212) 982-8895   themeatballshop.com

A ROUND TRIP

The Meatball Shop is not just a meatball restaurant; it's an observant meatball restaurant. Along with its regular meatballs, it makes holiday meatballs. If you don't eat them, you'll at least smile at them, and that's the idea. This is the shop that, one way or another, wants you to have a ball. "In the food world, everyone takes himself so seriously," says Daniel Holzman, the chef and cofounder of the shop. "We don't have to be so serious. We will cater to you in any way that we can; the one thing we ask when you walk in our doors is that you have a good time."

Not that you'd go to a place called The Meatball Shop to be grim, but a place by that name could call its balls "artisanal." This one doesn't. Instead, it calls them "naked," which you may not find any more appetizing, but playful is preferable to pretentious.

Playful reaches its pinnacle with the holiday balls, starting with the Jingle Balls, which are the Christmas balls, which, naturally, are made with reindeer. Likewise, Easter brings the Bunny Balls, which are made with rabbit, and Thanksgiving brings the Turkey Balls, which are served with Stuffing Balls.

But even the Naked Balls let you play, to the extent that you choose one ball type and one sauce, and mark your choices on a menu. You get four balls and focaccia bread. You can get sides like spaghetti. You can add a fried egg, which is called the Family Jewels. They never let up on the puns. The Naked Balls are Classic Beef, Spicy Pork, Chicken, Veggie, and the ball special. Almost all of the balls, including the beef, have pork, except for the Veggie. The sauces are Classic Tomato, Spicy Meat, Mushroom, Parmesan Cream, Pesto, and the sauce special.

You can instead get a Hero, which is three balls on a baguette with a sauce and either provolone or mozzarella cheese, or a Meatball Smash, which is two balls on a brioche bun with a sauce and a cheese. And for dessert you can have a homemade ice-cream sandwich, just because.

These meatballs were originally going to be sold from a window, as the meatballs are at Meatball Obsession, but that's another story. In this story, Daniel's mother introduces Daniel to Michael Chernow while Michael is on his rollerblades and Daniel is on his bike. The guys were 13 at the time.

They became friends, and then they became delivery boys for Candle Café, which is, amusingly, a vegan restaurant. Daniel grew up to be a chef at restaurants in California. Michael tended bars in New York. But it was all just prep for the balls.

Michael got Daniel to move back to New York to open the restaurant they'd dreamed of opening since they were on bikes and blades. They didn't know what kind of restaurant, but they found a vacant one with a window that faced a busy bar, and Michael was inspired. When he'd worked at the restaurant Frank, he liked its rigatoni ragù, which was pasta with meatballs, which he'd gotten without the pasta. "I said, 'When we open, we should sell something out of the window to drunk people.' Then we were walking around and I said, 'Hey, Dan—what do you think about meatballs?'"

They started cooking meatballs. Then the restaurant deal fell through. That gave them the time to decide to devote an entire restaurant to meatballs. "Nobody had really done meatballs," Michael says. "People thought it was funny, actually, and I think the comedy played into our success." They opened the first shop in 2010. They're up to six shops and 60 meatballs. Those include the Pizza Ball, the Jambalaya Ball, and, for St. Patrick's Day, the corned-beef-and-cabbage ball. Daniel creates the balls. And yet it's Michael who says: "I eat, breathe, sleep, dream, cry, and scream meatballs."

Other locations: 200 Ninth Ave., New York, NY 10011, (212) 257-4363; 64 Greenwich Ave., New York, NY 10014, (212) 982-7815; 447 Amsterdam Ave., New York, NY 10024, (212) 422-1752; 1462 Second Ave., New York, NY 10075, (212) 257-6121; 170 Bedford Ave., Brooklyn, NY 11249, (718) 551-0520

MELT BAKERY

132 Orchard St., New York, NY 10002
(646) 535-6358   meltbakery.com

ONE SWEET SANDWICH

Getting an ice-cream sandwich from a vending machine is like—well, getting a sandwich from a vending machine. You know it's a vending-machine sandwich, yet you eat it anyway. But that's something that you might never do again once you've eaten an ice-cream sandwich from Melt.

Julian Plyter couldn't make every snack food better, so he picked the one that arguably needed his help the most. The ice-cream sandwich is the neglected novelty. If you don't get it from a machine, you get it from a supermarket, which is almost the same thing.

An ice-cream-sandwich store might get the cold shoulder in most places, but it seemed to make perfect sense in New York City in 2012. The city had already gotten stores for practically every other kind of sandwich, and it had recently gotten a store for ice-cream pops. So Julian, who had envisioned opening a regular bakery, opened a bakery that sold only cookies sandwiching ice cream. He was prepared to do this because he'd already been selling his sandwiches from carts, alerting the city that these were everything the typical ones were not. Julian makes his cookies, which are round and have no holes. He makes his ice cream, in flavors other than vending-machine vanilla. He pairs the two in ways that they may never before have been paired. Even if you don't like cookies or ice cream, his sandwiches are nice to look at.

The signature is the Classic, which is chocolate-chip walnut cookies with vanilla ice cream. But then there's the Lovelet, which is red velvet "meltcakes" with cream-cheese ice cream. And on the dark side, there's the Morticia, which is "crackly" chocolate cookies with malted chocolate rum ice cream. Besides the Morticia, there's the Elvis, peanut-butter cookies

with banana ice cream. There's also the Cinnamax, snickerdoodles with cinnamon ice cream. And rounding out the regulars is the Thick Mint, which brings back the crackly chocolate cookies, this time with peppermint ice cream. Alternate choices have included the Big Whoop, chocolate meltcakes with buttercream ice cream; the Cocoa Daddy, brownie cookies with salted caramel ice cream; the Jack, molasses cookies with pumpkin-pie ice cream; and the Bold. That's salted-peanut cookies with beer ice cream.

As the menu suggests, Julian works in more than just flavors. "I really enjoy exploring textures in food," he says. Ice cream is generally creamy, but cookies have far more range: "I felt that with cookies, there was not an adequate representation of the available textures." So while the chocolate-chip cookies of the Classic are chewy, the red-velvet meltcakes of the Lovelet are cakey. The snickerdoodles are crispy-chewy. The peanut-butter cookies are sandy. The crackly cookies are crackly. The vending-machine cookies are soggy.

Julian, needless to say, is a pastry chef. He was working at Lever House Restaurant when he started making his sandwiches. He was on his way to opening a bakery in Inwood when he was stopped by Kareem Hamady, his business partner and, as it turned out, his good-idea man. Kareem urged Julian to stick to his sandwiches. So they sold the sandwiches at the Hester Street Fair and then from a cart on the High Line. In 2012, they opened the store. They sell sandwiches not only to passersby, but also to restaurants and to other stores.

They draw their menus from three dozen sandwiches, and besides inventing them, Julian likes naming them. The Jack, invented for Halloween, was named for the jack-o'-lantern, he says. And the Lovelet, invented for Valentine's Day, "is like a little love letter," in a meltcake envelope.

Other location: On the High Line, at W. 15th Street (seasonal)

MURRAY'S CHEESE BAR

264 Bleecker St., New York, NY 10014

(646) 476-8882   murrayscheesebar.com

FROMAGE TO YOU

For grilled cheese, there are grilled cheese places. For mac and cheese, there are mac and cheese places. But for a cheeseburger with your choice of cheddar, Gruyère, Fontina, Brie, rarebit cheddar sauce, three-cheese fondue, or creamy blue cheese—this is the place. It's not only the place for a breakfast, a lunch, or a dinner with cheese, but also the place for a breakfast, a lunch, or a dinner *of* cheese. It's the place for cheese plates, cheese snacks, cheese salads, cheese soups, cheese sides, cheese sausages, cheese biscuits, and cheese ice cream.

Outside there's a blackboard that says things like "From cheese to shining cheese!" Inside there's a showcase that tempts you with lots of cheese. If your usual cheeses have first names like cottage, cream, and Swiss, Murray's Cheese Bar will teach you how to make room for Challerhocker.

You'll find that cheese under Cheese a la Carte, in the Semi-Firm & Firm category, with the clarification "Switzerland/Raw Cow/Butterscotchy & Rich." If you prefer the Soft-Ripened category, you might instead make room for Prairie Fruits Farm Black Sheep ("Illinois/Sheep/Ashed, Luscious").

These are among the cheeses that appear in the Flights, which are plates of several cheeses and, if you're game, meats. The cheeses are chosen by cheese experts identified as cheesemongers, who know which cheeses you ought to like but will consider what you do like. Even if you don't take a Flight, you might want a Snack, like the Baked Bijou, which is goat-cheese buttons baked with mushrooms and "toasted bread." Or the most popular snack, Buffalo Cheese Curds, which are Wisconsin cheddar curds with Black River Blue Cheese dressing, and celery.

Come in early and start your day with, say, Alpine Eggs, which are poached eggs on an English muffin with ham, mushrooms, and three-cheese fondue. Come in later and break up your day with the cheeseburger, or maybe the mac and cheese, which is made with cheddar, Scharfe Maxx, Gruyère, and Gouda. Dinner can be the cheeseburger, the mac and cheese, or maybe the skirt steak, which comes with creamed spinach made with Nettle Meadow Kunik. Precede it, perhaps, with the French onion soup with a Challerhocker crouton. Follow it with the ice cream, in flavors like cheddar and Gouda.

New York couldn't go on forever without a place like this, but it was surely never imagined by the original big cheese. That was Murray Greenberg, who in 1940 opened Murray's Cheese Shop across the street. It's unlikely that Murray ever described a cheese as butterscotchy. In the '70s Murray sold the shop to his clerk Louis Tudda, who tailored it for what was then a heavily Italian neighborhood. In 1991 Louis passed the store to Rob Kaufelt, who came from a line of supermarket pioneers but somehow saw his future in cheese.

"I loved the Village," Rob says, "and I was happy to stand behind the counter with a couple of those old-time guys." But he didn't stand still. He moved the store, doubled its size, and transformed it into what today is often cited as the best cheese store in the city.

He also transformed Murray's into a national brand and transformed himself into a global cheese expert. He has published *The Murray's Cheese Handbook* and has set up a cheese school with classes like "Murray's Boot Camp" and "Feel the Funk! Exploring Stinky Cheese."

He sold grilled-cheese sandwiches at the store but had visions of a wine-and-cheese room. In 2012 he opened the inevitable Cheese Bar. But he still has visions. He was on a JetBlue plane when he purchased a "cheese snack box," he says. "We could do this better," he recalls thinking. "And it could say Murray's on it."

THE NUGGET SPOT

230 E. 14th St., New York, NY 10003

(646) 422-7346   thenuggetspot.com

CHICKEN UNCHAINED

Jason Hairston opened a little chicken-nugget restaurant a few steps away from a KFC. He saw his chicken restaurant and that chicken restaurant similar only in their use of the word "chicken." Needless to say, he's hoping that you'll see it that way, too.

It's hard not to, actually. Visit The Nugget Spot, for instance, then go to KFC and ask for a Twisted or a Cheez Louise. They may not send you back to The Nugget Spot, but neither will they fill your order, even if they do happen to know what you're talking about.

The Nugget Spot, which has not yet changed its name to TNS, is dedicated to putting more fun in your nuggets. It's even dedicated to putting more than chicken in your nuggets. Though it's built on a chicken foundation, it also has two vegetarian nuggets, one fish nugget, and one pig nugget.

Here there is no Colonel. There is just a Cap'n. It's Cap'n Crunk, the chicken nugget coated with sweet, crunchy cereal. It comes with Crunk Sauce, which is a spiced-butterscotch sauce. It's the perfect nugget for breakfast, lunch, and dinner, and for dessert at all three.

Apart from the military, there's Cheez Louise, the chicken nugget coated with crumbled cheese crackers and served with O.G. (Original Gangsta) Ranch Sauce. Also Twisted, the chicken nugget with pretzel crust and honey-mustard sauce, and the Southern Belle, the chicken nugget with Smokin' J's BBQ Sauce. Among non-chicken nuggets, there's The Grove, which is pork with coconut crust and Mambo Sauce, mambo being "soulful sweet & sour" sauce, and The Noodler, which is catfish with puffed-rice-and-Old-Bay-seasoning crust and Shhh Sauce, which is secret sauce.

There's also Po Po, a nugget of polenta, roasted tomatoes, and basil, with O.G. Ranch, and Mozzarella Nuggs, with Italian bread crumbs and Spicy Tomato Sauce. There are chicken nuggets over biscuits, chicken nuggets over waffles, and deep-fried pretzel-coated chocolate-chip-cookie-dough balls.

More than a nugget spot, it's a nugget world—which Jason created to keep himself at bay from the industrial world. He spent 10 years working at his grandfather's company, Bel-Bee Products, stamping out metal parts. It was a career that he felt the need to stamp out. He loved food, and he wanted to learn how to make it. He got jobs as a vegetable-chopper, a fry cook, and a line cook. He became sous chef at the Soho Grand Hotel, then at the Tribeca Grand Hotel. Then he was executive sous chef at Bobby Flay's Mesa Grill Bahamas.

Still, he wanted to be the boss. He just had to decide what he wanted to boss. He thought of wings, but they got nixed: "My younger sister said they're too messy for girls. My younger brother said every time he eats them, he has to wait twenty minutes before he touches anything." He moved on to nuggets, he says, because "who doesn't love nuggets? And there was certainly room for improvement." He began the improvements by creating his nugget sauces. The Nugget Spot opened in 2013, and within a few weeks it was attracting the long lines of success.

But Jason is still creating. He makes nuggets for holidays, like turkey nuggets for Thanksgiving and tortilla-chicken nuggets for Cinco de Mayo. "I made beer-batter chicken nuggets for Saint Patty's Day," he says. "I dyed 'em green. That didn't go over so well." He's added dark-meat chicken nuggets, which he calls a "pleasant surprise," and he's added Tso Tswag chicken nuggets as a Saturday special. He's working on baked chicken nuggets and on bacon-coated chicken nuggets. "You'd be surprised," he says, "at how many things work well with chicken nuggets."

OATMEALS

120 W. Third St., New York, NY 10012

(646) 360-3570   oatmealsny.com

HOT CEREAL

◎atmeal just needed some understanding. Samantha Stephens understood.

She understood that it was soothing. She understood that it was satisfying. But most of all she understood that it hadn't reached its potential. She realized that it was more than a heatable stand-in for Cheerios. She decided that she must nourish it, as it had nourished her.

Samantha knew that oatmeal could be more than just breakfast—specifically, it could be lunch, dinner, and dessert. So she dressed it with groupings like dried figs, crumbled Gorgonzola, and balsamic glaze. Then she gave it a place of its own, in the form of a restaurant she called OatMeals.

There you can start your day with a Tropical Sunrise, which is oatmeal with fresh pineapple, dried mango, toasted coconut, and coconut milk. Or with a Canadian, which is oatmeal with cinnamon roasted apples, sharp cheddar cheese, bacon, maple syrup, and sea salt. You can also end your day with those—if not with Strawberry Shortcake, which is oatmeal with graham crackers, strawberries, strawberry jelly, two sugars, and whipped cream. Or with Banana Cream Pie, which is oatmeal with Nilla Wafers, bananas, two sugars, and heavy cream.

OatMeals has 20 Signature Bowls, all of which make a nice meal, along with eight more called Happy Endings that could also make a nice meal. It has Bacon Pumpkin oatmeal, Pomegranate Pistachio oatmeal, Almond Joy oatmeal, and Lemon Meringue Pie oatmeal. It also has Build Your Own oatmeal, for people who think they can make order out of oatmeal and a hundred possible ingredients, which are in the categories of Fresh Fruit, Dried Fruit, Nuts & Seeds, Sweet Stuff, Savory Stuff, Milks, Spices, and Sweet

Dollops & Drizzles. Samantha will serve what you build—but, at least in dire cases, she will gently try to guide you toward a Signature Bowl. She won't say it herself, but she is nothing short of an oatmeal genius. The best thing she ever paired with oatmeal is herself.

She was an executive assistant in equity research at J.P. Morgan when she began to think that her future was in a bowl. She'd already met her muse while majoring in psychology at Baruch College: "I started eating oatmeal because it was cheap, and I was on a budget, and it was good for you." She took classes at NYU and learned about business. She attended the French Culinary Institute and came out a pastry chef. She knew she wanted a restaurant and she couldn't let go of oatmeal, though some understandably concerned friends did their best to loosen her grip. It took her 10 years, but she opened OatMeals in 2012 and was greeted with delight, if a degree of bafflement. For the resistant, she was ready with sandwiches, though all of them on oatmeal bread, and a line of treats—like Oatmeal Bread Pudding and Swedish Chocolate Oat Balls.

She wasn't open long before Quaker Oats came around. Its people wisely believed they could profit from the creativity of an oatmeal genius. Samantha has since been designated Quaker's Creative Oatmeal Officer, "to bring unexpected oat ideas to you." Now she's really feeling her oats. There seems no limit to where oatmeal can take her, even beyond being named a Creative Oatmeal Officer. She talks of OatMeals products, of an OatMeals cookbook, of an OatMeals in Midtown, and of oatmeal bars in airports, in malls, and on college campuses.

Meanwhile, she's still in her store inventing new bowls. Lately she's added one called Devils Off Horseback. It has goat cheese, bacon, dates, sliced almonds, and maple syrup. "I'm really surprised at how well goat cheese works in oatmeal," she says. "It's beautiful."

OTAFUKU × MEDETAI

220 E. Ninth St., New York, NY 10003
(646) 998-3438   otafukuny.com

HAPPY COMBINATION

◎ tafuku x Medetai spotlights four foods, but three are forms of pancakes, and all four are Japanese street foods. And it's for the best, because while two of the four could be considered meals, one of the four is a dessert, and one of the four is grilled octopus balls.

None of the four is Otafuku. Otafuku is the Goddess of Mirth. She makes people happy, which is why the restaurant chose her as its symbol. None of the four is medetai either. *Medetai* is a word that means "happiness," which is why the restaurant uses it as another name for one of the foods.

That food is taiyaki, the one that's a dessert. It's a crisp, fluffy pancake filled with red bean paste or chocolate-hazelnut spread and banana. More important, it's shaped like a red snapper, a fish that's a symbol of happiness. If nothing else, Otafuku x Medetai takes a positive attitude. The taiyaki, also known as medetai, was added to the menu when the restaurant moved from a smaller spot in 2014. The original spot had the other three foods, two of them also pancakes: okonomiyaki, also known as Japanese pizza, and takoyaki, also known as octopus balls.

Takoyaki, which is not to be confused with taiyaki, are octopus-pancake balls covered with "special sauce," mayonnaise, and bonito flakes. They're crispy on the outside and doughy on the inside. The octopus is on the inside. Okonomiyaki are savory pancakes with shredded cabbage and shrimp or pork, also topped off with special sauce, mayonnaise, and bonito flakes. They are crunchy on the outside and soft on the inside. They sometimes stood in for rice during the Second World War. The fourth food is yakisoba, chewy noodles with special sauce, shrimp, cabbage, and scallions, topped with red ginger and dried seaweed. Though they are Japanese noodles,

they are said to have descended from Chinese noodles. You get a lot of culinary history here.

In Japan, okonomiyaki and takoyaki are common in restaurants as well as at street stands and at fairs and festivals. In New York, though, they are pretty scarce. So as long as they're in one place, people often want to try both, and maybe the others. The place has a plan.

Combo A combines takoyaki and taiyaki. Combo B combines takoyaki and okonomiyaki. Combo C combines takoyaki and yakisoba. Combo D combines yakisoba and okonomiyaki. Combo A combined with Combo D combines takoyaki, taiyaki, yakisoba, and okonomiyaki.

These opportunities are brought to you by Bon Yagi, who has been bringing Japanese food to New York for 35 years. He came here in 1968 and started out delivering vegetables. In 1980 he opened an edgy diner called 103 Second. But that was just his appetizer. He started building his Japanese empire in 1984 with Hasaki, which still stars sushi, sashimi, and sake. Since then he has come up with a series of places that spotlight assorted Japanese specialties, some of which rarely get time in the spotlight. They include Shabu-Tatsu, featuring shabu-shabu, a Japanese hotpot; Curry-Ya, featuring Japanese curry; Soba-Ya, featuring Japanese buckwheat noodles; Rai Rai Ken, a ramen bar; Decibel and Sakagura, both sake bars; Hi-Collar, a coffee bar; and Cha-An, a teahouse.

Most of the spots are in the East Village, where Bon has more or less built what's unofficially known as Little Tokyo. And he keeps building. Late in 2014 he opened Yonekichi, which sells rice burgers—in which the rice is the bun—in the former home of Otafuku.

PAPAYA KING

179 E. 86th St., New York, NY 10028

(212) 369-0648   papayaking.com

TROPICAL ESCAPE

Some culinary singles are couples—Mac and Cheese, Fish and Chips, Wafels and Dinges—and indisputably greater together than they were apart. Papaya King is the birthplace of one of the greatest couples in New York culinary history: Frankfurters and Tropical Fruit Drinks. The frankfurters are tasty but they become even tastier when accompanied by a frothy cup of papaya, mango, or banana. The exact ingredients of the drinks are as imponderable as the exact ingredients of the dogs, but that may be for the best. Everyone loves a good mystery.

The original stand, on 86th Street, dates to 1932. It's been gussied up, but it still captures the Papaya King of old. It does this mostly by imparting information about its foods, which mostly suggests that you can leave the place healthier than you were when you came in. "Take a moment & appreciate how lucky you are," your papaya-drink cup instructs modestly. "You're holding sixteen fluid ounces of 100% bona-fide deliciousness. Made with papaya, the aristocratic melon of the tropics. Known as a nutritional masterpiece."

The cup goes on to proclaim the fruit's power to control aging, promote heart health, and improve male fertility. Where the cup stops, the room takes over, in signature yellow signs that announce things like: "Mangoes offer among the highest amount of beta carotene of any fruit." Thus assured that the restaurant is committed to your well-being, you can choose your meal with confidence that it will restore you, whether you have your hot dogs with sauerkraut, mustard, relish, coleslaw, sweet pickles, cheddar cheese, chili, or fried onions.

Your traditional drink choices include Papaya, Mango, Coconut Champagne, Piña Colada, Strawberry Fields, and Banana Daquiri. These have been joined by fruit smoothies, which go by the names of Papaya Pride, Pineapple Surprise, and Banana Berry.

There are also fries and knishes. But the kingdom was built on fruit. It was the fruit that beguiled Gus Poulos when he was vacationing in Miami (or Cuba). Gus, who was from Greece, was running a deli in New York, where, at the time, papayas and mangoes were tough to come by.

Determined to change that, he opened a stand selling Floridian tropical drinks, which he nevertheless chose to name Hawaiian Tropical Drinks. The drinks tanked. So Gus had girls in hula skirts give them away. Business improved, as it does when girls in hula skirts get involved. Still, Gus chose a German girlfriend, by the name of Birdie. She fed him German food, including frankfurters. Gus thought that they'd pair nicely with fruit drinks, and that he'd pair nicely with Birdie. His devotion to fruit thus resulted in two historic marriages.

Through the years Gus opened other stands, some in other cities. Along the way, it is said, a Brooklyn Dodger called him the papaya king. He liked the name. He took it. Others guys were taken with it. They launched stands with names like Papaya Kingdom, Papaya Paradise, and Papaya Prince.

One of those stands, Gray's Papaya, has become a landmark of its own. Most of the others have come and gone, including the other Papaya Kings. But in 2013 the latest owners of Papaya King opened a branch on St. Mark's Place. It has not only the yellow signs, but also a concrete porch.

Though the stands have left the Poulos family, the food still seems the same. Except that now it includes deep-fried Oreos, Twinkies, and Moon Pies. "It's a totally different category, but it's a delicious dessert," says Wayne Rosenbaum, the director of operations. "It's sweet. Just like our drinks."

Other location: 3 St. Mark's Place, New York, NY 10003, (646) 692-8482

PEANUT BUTTER & CO.

240 Sullivan St., New York, NY 10012

(212) 677-3995   ilovepeanutbutter.com

THE NUTTIEST DREAM

They didn't laugh when Lee Zalben announced that he would open a peanut-butter-sandwich restaurant. This was most likely because Lee Zalben didn't announce it. "I didn't tell many people, 'cause I knew it was such a crazy idea," he says. "I knew if I shared it with too many people, I was gonna hear too much negativity. I also knew that—as much as I explained it—until they walked in the door, they weren't gonna get it. This included my mother."

So far, his restaurant has lasted 17 years. Meanwhile, his peanut butter has landed in 15,000 stores. Peanut Butter & Co. is a beacon for people who are searching for a great spread and a guidepost for people who are following in its audaciously singular footsteps.

"When I look at the restaurant landscape, it's gratifying and exciting to know that I've been a trailblazer when it comes to niche food concepts in New York," Lee says. "And it's very gratifying to bring people so much happiness, pleasure, and joy. No one leaves Peanut Butter and Company unhappy." It would be hard to, unless you have the peanut allergy. The restaurant is like home, except with more sandwich ingredients. "What we tried to create," Lee told me back when the place opened, "is a cross between an old-fashioned country store, a schoolroom, and Mom's kitchen."

Within the sunny yellow walls, you can regress with peanut butter and jelly, peanut butter and Nutella, or perhaps a nice Fluffernutter. Or you can move on to, say, peanut butter with vanilla cream cheese and chocolate chips, or grilled peanut butter with bananas and honey. That would be The Elvis. You can plumb the Gourmet sandwiches, which begin with spicy peanut butter with grilled chicken and pineapple jam, and which also include

cinnamon-raisin peanut butter with vanilla cream cheese and apple slices, and maple peanut butter with bacon.

There's also a PB&J of the Week, like the Strawberry Shortcake, which is white-chocolate peanut butter with strawberry jam and Fluff. And there are peanut-butter cookies, brownies, sundaes, parfaits, and pies, which are called desserts, though it's hard to tell the difference.

Everything's made with Peanut Butter & Co. peanut butter, whose 10 flavors do include just plain Smooth and just plain Crunchy. Every sandwich is served with carrot sticks and potato chips on Fiesta plates, which sometimes disappear in the hands of patrons with sticky fingers.

But then, it all started with sticky fingers. Lee got them from the family peanut-butter jar, which is why his mother assigned him a jar of his own. At Vassar College, he won late-night peanut-butter competitions by mixing in stuff like dried apricots, Grape-Nuts, and Hershey bars. He was doing time in advertising when he passed his future storefront, and instantly recognized it as his future storefront. The next day he quit his job. He did freelance work while making a business plan for the restaurant whose theme he judiciously wouldn't reveal. The restaurant opened in 1998, which indeed made it a pioneer in the new generation of single-food spots. Baffled patrons came in and ordered alternatives like the chicken salad, but they were followed by peanut-butter people who often traded peanut-butter memories.

Lee's never had build-your-own sandwiches, but he has taken requests, like the one that came from a hungry mother-to-be. "She wanted peanut butter and pickles," he says, "and was shocked that we didn't have it." He ran out for pickles. He tried the sandwich. It's on the menu as the Pregnant Lady.

Not all requests get that far, though. "A lot of them involve peanut butter and onions," Lee says. "People tell us how their grandparents ate peanut butter and onions, or peanut butter and mayo. There are a lot of grandparents out there who ate peanut-butter-and-onion sandwiches."

PETITE SHELL

1269 Lexington Ave., New York, NY 10028

(212) 828-2233

EASY FOR YOU TO SAY

Never have so many loved a pastry that so few can pronounce.

Rugelach—which commonly begins with a *rug*, not a *roog*, and ends with a guttural *lakh*, not a *la*—are just one of those creations that people can't seem to help loving, even if the pastry lacks the prominence, along with the pronounceability, of cookies, cake, and pie.

Among those who love rugelach is Shmilly Gruenstein, who decided to address both of the pastry's disadvantages. For prominence, he gave it a restaurant, on the Upper East Side. For pronounceability, he gave it an alternate name, which he also gave to the restaurant: Petite Shell.

The first surprise at Petite Shell for people familiar with rugelach is that a name like "petite shell" could refer to rugelach. The second surprise at Petite Shell for many people familiar with rugelach is that the petite shells are not the rugelach that they are familiar with.

They are not the little strudelian mounds that are typically filled with nuts along with chocolate or a fruit jam like raspberry or apricot. They are little crescents that, accordingly, look less like, say, potato puffs than like croissants, a pastry that might be their progeny.

They are the rugelach that were brought here by Eastern European Jews and the rugelach that Shmilly wanted to share. "I grew up with it," he says. "It's a treat that we had every Shabbos morning. That's what we woke up to. We had it with milk, and the adults had it with coffee."

Having since turned into an adult, he's become partial to the coffee. "People have eaten coffee and pastries together for centuries," he says. The concept of Petite Shell, then, is actually "fine and exceptional coffee with fine and exceptional pastry. You can't separate the two."

Whether you can or not, the pastry comes in flavors that probably were not brought here by Eastern European Jews. They include white-chocolate apple, blue-cheese pear, raspberry and farmer cheese, dulce de leche, pecorino tomato, feta kalamata olive, and jalapeño cream cheese.

Along with the shells, Shmilly has added what are billed as croissant sandwiches but which could be considered rugelach sandwiches. They include the Brie Apple, with honey and walnuts; the Blue-Cheese Fig, with apple and pistachios; the Goat-Cheese Avocado, with tomato and horse-radish; the Mozzarella Pesto, with tomato and olives; and the Manchego Breakfast, with avocado, omelette, and salsa.

As for the coffee, it's roasted by Forty Weight Coffee Roasters and brewed in a Steampunk brewer, all of which is not jive to the javaphile. This is what's known as third-wave coffee, which is the wave of coffee meant, as Shmilly puts it, "to be appreciated like wine."

The shop's refinement notwithstanding, Shmilly's background is in investing. He styles himself neither barista nor baker, but venture capitalist. He became a proprietor, he says, through a connection he made while try-ing to work out a deal for a franchisee of a national fro-yo chain.

In 2013 he opened a rugelach shop in Brooklyn. "It had the same prod-uct," he says, "but the execution was very poor." He found a partner who knew marketing, and he opened Petite Shell in 2015. "The execution," he says, "went from poor to perfect."

As for the name, that came from the partner. "The pastry looks like a seashell," Shmilly says, "and that conjures up memories of childhood sum-mers spent on the beach. And shells often have surprises inside, and we built in a pocket of extra filling, so we're hiding a surprise inside."

That said, he didn't like the name. "But I'm choosing my battles," he says. He trusted in his partner's wisdom—and it seems to be paying off. "People walk in, and there's love," Shmilly says. "They love the place; they love the product. That's the beauty of food. If you get it right, it hits people."

PIADA

601 Lexington Ave., New York, NY 10022
(212) 752-2727 piadanyc.com

LESS IS MORE

Piada won't necessarily make you feel like you're in a Fellini movie, although it might make you feel like you're in six Fellini movies. The director was born in the same place as the restaurant's namesake sandwich, so the restaurant named its sandwiches after his films. Of course, there are people around who don't know who Fellini is, but that really isn't much of a problem for the restaurant. What is a problem is that there are people around who don't know what a piada is, which actually can make them feel like they're in a Fellini movie.

"The biggest problem we face is how to explain what piadina is," says Giovanni Attilio, using the sandwich's alternate name to confuse you. "You look at it, it looks like a tortilla or pita, so you have an idea. But it's the wrong idea. You think it's about the bread. But it's about the ingredients."

The bread is round and flat. The ingredients are piquant. They work together to give you an uncommon sandwich experience. They've been doing this for perhaps centuries, in what's now the Emilia-Romagna region of Italy, where they're still sold from kiosks and carts by piadinaros.

But while a piada is an Italian sandwich, it's not an American Italian sandwich. "It's not like a meatball sandwich, for example," Giovanni says. "People have in mind this idea of an Italian sandwich with a lot of stuff. Piadina is the opposite. It has fewer ingredients, so you can taste all of them." The best way to illustrate is to go to the movies, starting with the first one on the menu, *Amarcord*. It's made with prosciutto di Parma, mozzarella, and arugula. "The salty prosciutto," Giovanni says, "contrasts with the sweet mozzarella, which contrasts with the peppery arugula." Fini.

Similar direction guides *Lo Sceicco Bianco*, which contains prosciutto cotto, stracchino, and arugula; *Notti di Cabiria*, with mortadella, parmigiano, and tomato; *La Strada*, with salame, pecorino, and balsamic vinegar; and *La Dolce Vita*, with bresaola, parmigiano, and arugula. The menu winds up with Giulietta, named for Fellini's wife, Giulietta Masina, and made with tomato, mozzarella, and basil; Federico, named for Fellini himself, made with grilled eggplant, pepper, zucchini, and basil; and *Satyricon*, named for that movie, made with speck, Fontina, and tomato.

In style, of course, Fellini was the opposite of piada; his films are famous for being complex, if not bizarre. Perhaps in homage to this, Piada presents Make Your Own Piada, in which you choose your own ingredients from lists of meats, cheeses, and vegetables.

But it was the traditional piada that Giovanni thought should have a home here. He grew up near the piada's home in Italy. His grandmother made piade. His mother made piade. About a decade ago, he started thinking maybe he should make piade. "I was traveling in the US," he says. "I realized I can't find this kind of sandwich. I was wondering why." His business partners didn't know. One night they all talked about a shop. "I thought, no way I'm gonna do it. I didn't sleep all night. The next day I said, 'When do we start?'"

Giovanni joined with Daniele Buraschi and Andrea Tagliazucchi to open Piada on the Lower East Side in 2005. The response persuaded them to try a bigger spot in a busier area. They moved the store to Midtown in 2009, and it was joined by a branch at The Plaza in 2014.

The make-your-own option was added by request, Giovanni says. But a true piada, he cautions, should have four ingredients, tops. When people pile on, he lives with it. "We don't mind," he says. "We are in America. And they are used to doing that. They can eat what they want."

Other location: The Plaza Food Hall, 1 W. 59th St., New York, NY 10019, (347) 481-7311

THE PICKLE GUYS

49 Essex St., New York, NY 10002
(212) 656-9739   pickleguys.com

BRINING IN STYLE

A pickle is often something you get whether you want it or not, which is why the pickle you get is often not a pickle you want. It's the sliver drowning in the ketchup puddle atop a glossy slider, or the spear face-down in the coleslaw clump served as a diner perk, or the refugee from the aging jar glued to a fridge-door shelf, or, saddest of all, the lumpy mash in the squeeze bottle mockingly labeled "relish." These less-than-virgin forms can easily make you forget that the pickle can be an appealing food when it's made and presented with pride. It can be appetizing, tasty, and firm. It can be in one piece. You can still revisit these truths with a visit to The Pickle Guys.

The Pickle Guys is Pickle's Last Stand, at least in the pickle district, a part of the Lower East Side that was home to dozens of pickle vendors. The district dates back a century, when it was founded by Jewish immigrants. It lives on thanks to Alan Kaufman, the Pickle Guys president. "I'm Jewish. I love pickles," Alan says. "People take a bite of my product and say, 'That's a great pickle.' You don't get that in too many jobs. People thank me for being here. You don't get that in too many jobs. I'd like to keep the place around for another sixty years."

Alan purveys his pickles from the traditional barrels, even if the barrels must now be nontraditional plastic. He has the traditional new pickles, sour pickles, half-sour pickles, three-quarters-sour pickles, pickled tomatoes, pickled peppers, pickled watermelon, and pickled herring. He also has hot new pickles, hot sour pickles, horseradish pickles, pickled tomatillos, pickled okra, pickled string beans, pickled garlic, pickled mushrooms, pickled celery, pickled carrots, pickled turnips, pickled baby corn, pickled

beets, and seven kinds of olives. He displays around three dozen barrels of pickled things, which, by the way, also include pickled mango and pickled pineapple. These duly impress the visitors from around the country and the world who come to see pickles in their natural habitat and to get a taste of a bygone life.

Alan makes the pickles in the store, with bygone recipes. What you get, he says, is "flavor, texture, and snap. When you bite that pickle, it's gotta snap. If you take a pickle and bend it end-to-end and it doesn't snap, it just bends, it's a weak pickle. Nobody wants a weak pickle." That was doubtless among the precepts that guided the Jewish pickle guys on the Lower East Side at the turn of the last century. Many Jews turned to pickles not only because pickles were old-country favorites, but also because they were cheap to make, to sell, and to buy.

The stars of local pickle history were Izzy Guss and Louis Hollander, whose rivalry may have been sour but reportedly led to better pickles. Guss' Pickles survived in the district until 2009, although, through its later decades, it changed addresses and owners. Guss history lives on through the latter-day Guss' Pickles on Long Island and through Clinton Hill Pickles in Brooklyn, run by the last owner of the city store, but the pickle presence in the pickle district belongs to The Pickle Guys—whose principal pickle guy is a graduate of Guss'.

Alan worked for both Hollander and Guss, and at Guss he was a pickle maker and later a manager. He took a detour into advertising photography but disliked the down time. He decided to run his own pickle store, which he suspected would leave little down time.

He likes the tradition. He likes the appreciation of the tradition. He tells a tale of that appreciation without naming any names: "People come here and buy three pickles in a bag. Then they go to a famous place and eat my pickles instead of theirs. It happens all the time."

Other location: 1364 Coney Island Ave., Brooklyn, NY 11230, (718) 677-0639

POMMES FRITES

Address in transition

(212) 674-1234   pommesfritesnyc.com

TAKE A DIP

Fries are the one food in New York that you'd probably have to work not to find. Yet every day people line up to get the fries at Pommes Frites. One reason is that the place is so little that two people make a line. But another is that these fries are among the most prized snacks in the city. They are not the fries of your neighborhood diner, tavern, or burgeria. They are the fries of the little fry shops that pepper the world's fry capital, Belgium. These fries are fried two times, making them crunchy and fluffy, and come with flavored mayonnaise, making you forget about ketchup.

There is ketchup, if you must, but if you want to understand why there's a line, you mustn't. Instead, you must pay a bit extra and get one of The Tasty Sauces, which you're unlikely to find at your neighborhood diner, tavern, or burgeria. That is, unless one of those serves Sweet Mango Chutney Mayo, Smoked Eggplant Mayo, or Pomegranate Teriyaki Mayo. Or Wasabi Mayo, Horseradish Mayo, Pesto Mayo, Lemon Dill Mayo, Rosemary Garlic Mayo, or Vietnamese Pineapple Mayo.

Say no to mayo and you can still choose from, say, Blue Cheese, Cheddar Cheese, Mexican Ketchup, Curry Ketchup, Peanut Satay, and Irish Curry. Say no to the extra buck-fifty, and besides ketchup, you can have, say, mustard, Tabasco, malt vinegar, or Frites Sauce (aka European Mayo). It's a perpetual fry festival, or at least perpetual since it opened in 1997. Similar stands, with names like B. Frites and Chipsy, have come and gone. Even another branch of Pommes Frites has come and gone. But the original keeps going, maybe because it's the original.

Pommes Frites was the inspiration of Suzanne Levinson, who was inspired not because she was a chef or an entrepreneur, but because she was hungry. She was a Bronx girl studying art history in Europe through Ohio University when she came upon the frites shops of the Netherlands and Belgium. She had fries, she says, "and I thought, 'This is the best thing I've ever had.'" She also thought that if *she* thought so, other New Yorkers would think so, too. She asked a friend if she should open a fry stand in Manhattan. "She said, 'If you don't do it, someone else will.'"

She took a job with a European tour operator, which kept bringing her back to those fries, and she eventually succumbed to her need to bring the fries back to New York. She talked to experts, raised money, drew up a business plan, opened her shop, and instantly recognized that she was in over her head. Within two months, she took on a partner named Omer Shorshi. Within two years, they opened a second stand, in Times Square. It didn't work out. In Times Square, people apparently are not in the market for Organic Black Truffle Mayo or even Bordeaux, Fig & Sage Mayo.

Eventually, though, they opened something else that worked out: Frite shop.com, which sells Belgian-fry supplies. It offers imported paper and cardboard cones in dozens of styles and sizes. These days, Omer mostly tends to the frites shop, and Suzanne mostly sells the supplies.

If that makes Suzanne sound ambivalent, it's because she is. With uncommon candor, she suggests that customers go easy on her food. "It's really quite unhealthy," she says. "I tell people to split their orders and to limit their visits. When I got into this, I was a stupid twenty-year-old."

Still, if you're going to risk-take, you might as well go all the way, which is why Suzanne encourages people to sample her sauces. "Harrison Ford came in," she says. "I thought he would be so adventurous—'cause he's Indiana Jones. He just got barbecue. I thought, 'Did you have to take that away from me?'"

Note: Pommes Frites, which was in the East Village for 18 years, was among the stores destroyed by a gas explosion in March 2015. At press time, the owners were planning to reopen in the fall, at 128 MacDougal Street in Greenwich Village.

POPBAR

5 Carmine St., New York, NY 10014

(212) 255-4874   pop-bar.com

TASTE THE RAINBOW

Welcome. Today, as you can see, we have red, orange, yellow, green, purple, and pink. Which one will you have?

At Popbar, this is not what they say, but in way, it's what you hear. You hear it from a polychromatic profusion of pops. A display case holds several hundred of them, standing up in perfect rows like rectangular soldiers, all with sticks coming out of their heads. You could look at the list of flavors but you probably won't for a while, since you're looking down at the colors and imagining what flavors they are. Flavors are the main draw, but the case is the main attraction, because it tells you that you have come upon the ultimate shop for pops.

They are not precisely ice-cream pops. They are gelato pops and sorbetto pops, the sorbetto pops being the ones in most of the pretty colors. On any day, you can choose from about two dozen flavors—out of about four dozen—and you can always see what you're choosing. "Our major rule is to always look at things from different points of view," says Reuben Ben-Jehuda, one of Popbar's founders. "We always take a look from the front. People choose not by menu but by display. They'll say, 'Tell me what it is, but I'm gonna have it anyway.'"

Just for the record, the popSorbettos come in apricot, banana, blood orange, grapefruit, lemon, mandarin orange, mango, mixed berry, mixed berry peach, orange, peach, pineapple, strawberry, strawberry pineapple split, and strawberry diagonally dipped in dark chocolate, which is especially pretty.

The popGelatos, however, get far more complex, and they come mostly in shades of brown and white, which means that unless you really don't care, you must give them more serious study, or else you could end up with peanut butter when you meant to have coffee. The basic flavors are banana, chocolate, coconut, coffee, cream, gianduia, hazelnut, mint, peanut butter, pistachio, and vanilla. The basics also form the bases of myPops (of which the dipped strawberry popSorbetto is one), which are dipped in chocolate and sometimes in what are called "poppings."

The myPops include banana, coffee, or vanilla fully dipped in dark chocolate; chocolate fully dipped in white chocolate; vanilla fully dipped in milk chocolate; hazelnut with chopped hazelnuts half-dipped in dark chocolate; and vanilla fully dipped in dark-chocolate sprinkles. If that's not enough—and it isn't, since it doesn't include chocolate dipped in dark chocolate—there is also the custom-built myPop. You pick a basic, then pick a chocolate dip and, if you like, poppings. The other poppings, besides the ones mentioned, are almonds, granola, and coffee grains.

All of this is what Reuben considers simple—or at least did when he and his partner, Daniel Yaghoubi, came up with the idea. "We were trying to figure out how to offer something unique in a city that has everything," he says, "but we wanted something that would not need a big operation."

Daniel grew up in Germany and loved his family's homemade ice pops. Reuben grew up in Italy and loved his country's homemade gelato. They became friends through their families, and after their families moved to New York, it was a matter of time before they'd team up to put gelato on a stick. They opened Popbar in 2010 and have since followed the New York store with others, including five in Jakarta, Indonesia. As they add locations, they add ideas; they've introduced wafflePops, popBites, and Hot Chocolate on a Stick, which, Reuben says, you can "eat and drink at the same time."

They also have seasonal specials, like the Pumpkin Pie popGelato. And yet, as is often the case, the bestsellers are the classics. "Last summer, we did avocado," Reuben says. "It gets people in and talking. And then they might choose just plain old vanilla or chocolate."

gianduia
popGelato

strawberry
popSorbetto

pistachio
popGelato

dulce de leche
popGelato

mixed berries
popSorbetto

blood orange
popSorbetto

banana
popGelato

PORCHETTA

110 E. Seventh St., New York, NY 10009
(212) 777-2151   porchettanyc.com

TASTEFUL PIG

Porchetta is sometimes regarded as the Italian pulled pork, which is exactly how not to regard it if you've never had porchetta. It's roasted pork that is succulent and savory, but it isn't barbecue. If you want barbecued pulled pork, you're better off in South Carolina. If you want porchetta, however, you're better off at Porchetta, the place that's been showing the city what its namesake is about. It sells porchetta in a sandwich, porchetta on a plate, and little else, except for the cooking greens and white beans that come on the plate.

Porchetta is the creation of Sara Jenkins and Matt Lindemulder, who are cousins and who as such ate porchetta together in Rome when they were children. The taste lingered long enough to inspire them to go into business together selling an Italian street food that was nearly obscure in New York. "Porchetta was something we both loved," Matt says, "and porchetta was something nobody else was doing in the traditional way, which was the way we wanted to do it." The store opened in 2008, and by the end of the year *Time Out New York* named its sandwich the best thing to eat in the city.

Porchetta's porchetta is not strictly traditional. It's made with half a pig, whereas the Italian version is made with an entire pig. Sara says she went half-hog partly for space and partly for looks: "We thought it would freak Americans out to come and see a great big grinning pig head." Italian porchetta begins with a whole pig that's been boned, gutted, and restuffed with stuff like its heart, its spleen, and its liver. It's salted and otherwise seasoned, rolled up, and roasted over wood. It's typically sold from trucks and stands. It's a happy hand food.

At Porchetta, they skip to the loin, or the hip to the shoulder, take out the bones, and stuff it with garlic, rosemary, sage, and wild fennel pollen. The organs stay out—again in deference to a different public: "The American palette is not as accustomed to offal stuffing," Matt says. The loin is wrapped in belly and scored skin, rolled, tied, and slow-cooked in an oven. What comes out is a golden bundle of flavors and textures. "You get the fattiness of the belly, the juiciness of the loin, and the crunchiness of the skin," Matt says. That's what *Time Out New York* tasted.

That's also what Sara tasted as a kid living in Rome, which was one of many cities she lived in as the daughter of a foreign correspondent. When she was visited by her cousin Matt, they tasted it together. It could be why they both eventually set out for careers in food. Sara became a chef, worked at several city restaurants, and wrote a cookbook, with Mindy Fox, called *Olives & Oranges*. Matt preferred the front jobs, and got those in several restaurants. Both wanted a place of their own—and they made a perfect match.

Sara, however, soon needed to get her hands back on more foods, so in 2010 she opened Porsena, an Italian spot down the street. That left Matt on his own at Porchetta. He misses his cousin's company, but he has plenty of other people around to keep him occupied.

"We had one woman come in, and she left quite offended and upset," he says. "She wanted the pig skull, and she thought we were hiding it from her. She said, 'How can you not have the pig head? I know you have it. You have it, and you're not giving it to me.'" There was also the Italian man who, not unlike a few others, scoffed at this refined dish cooked up by two non-Italians. "He looked down his nose at us," Matt says. "He said, 'I know porchetta. This is not porchetta.' I got him a sandwich, and he came in every day for the next week."

POTATOPIA

378 Sixth Ave., New York, NY 10011

(212) 260-4100   potatopia.com

UNDERGROUND HIT

On a wall of Potatopia is the directive "Get Smashed," which might sound like a call to debauchery but which is actually a serving suggestion. It's a message that tells you that this is not a baked-potato stand but rather a full-line potato restaurant, at which getting Smashed is only one option. You can get Smashed. You can get Curly. You can get Skin Chip, Shoestring, or Au Gratin. You can get Potato Chip; you can get Sweet Potato Crinkle. You can get not only Baked Potato, but also Baked Sweet Potato, and when you've decided which potato to get, the getting has only begun.

Since, by getting a potato, you have chosen to Build Your Own, you can get one or more of 16 toppings, including five different cheeses. You can get a "protein," meaning shrimp, chicken, steak, bacon, or sausage, and you can get one of 14 sauces. Sour cream is a sauce. If you don't see yourself as a builder, you can still get. After all, this is the potato utopia. You can choose from the Signature Meals, in which the ingredients have already been gotten. There are six of those, containing as many as 15 toppings and sauces. The one with 15 toppings and sauces is called the Comatoser, which, despite the name, does not involve getting Smashed. It is Skin Chips, with salt, pepper, cheddar cheese, Asiago cheese, pepper jack cheese, green onions, red onions, garlic, cilantro, jalapeño, broccoli, bacon, melted cheddar, roasted pepper aioli, and ranch. Ranch is also a sauce.

All of this was invented by Allen Dikker, who suitably did his inventing in Edison, New Jersey. An ad man with a knack for sauces, he opened his first store in 2011 in the Menlo Park Mall, partly as an out-of-town tryout for a store in New York.

He picked potatoes, he says, because "everything else is out there." But of course, potatoes have long since been out there. The oldest store in this book, Yonah Schimmel Knish Bakery, has been selling potato knishes since 1910, and Yonah sold his knishes from a cart before that. One of the most successful single-food shops in New York is Pommes Frites, which for decades has been selling nothing but fries. And people have sold baked potatoes from carts for well over a century. One guy ran a string of potato carts that looked like little locomotives.

What Allen added were infinite options—which can be a liability, since there are still people who get overwhelmed by infinite options. But if they love a potato, Allen says, they eventually acclimate, even if, on their first visit, they flee without digging in.

For dining in, the store is more utilitarian than utopian, but Allen did allow for a little fun with spuds. The door has a potato-shaped hand hole, the fountains have potato handles, and the wall, besides saying "Get Smashed," says "Get Baked," "Get Sauced," and "Get Fried."

Most people, as it turns out, seem to want to get Smashed. The Smashed Hit is the most popular Signature Meal. It's Smashed Potato with salt, pepper, cheddar cheese, Asiago cheese, green onions, red onions, garlic, cilantro, and roasted pepper aioli. It's just a few toppings short of a Comatoser.

Potatopia understandably promotes the nutritional advantages of potatoes. Just remember that those advantages fluctuate with your toppings and sauces. The store points out, for example, that a potato has no cholesterol, but that's only before it becomes a Comatoser or a Smashed Hit.

RICE TO RICHES

37 Spring St., New York, NY 10012

(212) 274-0008   ricetoriches.com

PUNCH-LINE PUDDING

Those who dwell on the success of rice pudding as a solo food are over-looking the success of rice pudding as a solo act. The pudding long ago made a name for itself as a dessert, but only at Rice to Riches has it made a name for itself as a stand-up comedian.

Not that it stands up. But it's good for a laugh. It speaks through the dozens of signs that are hanging up all over its store. They say things like "Think with your stomach," "Anything worth eating is worth overeating," and most mercilessly, "Eat all you want . . . you're already fat." People read the signs, figure they make good sense, and scarf down the pudding, usually 8 or 12 ounces at a time. They leave gratified, and proud of it. As one sign says, "Never diet on an empty stomach." As another says, "Eat right, exercise, die anyway."

"I like to pay attention to all five senses," says Pete Moceo, the creator of Rice to Riches and the rice's head writer. "Walking in here should be like walking into a theater. I look at Rice to Riches as a whole experience. We gave rice pudding a complete makeover."

Whatever you think of his messages, his statement is accurate. Rice pudding has never been on this kind of a roll. The store opened in 2003 and has become an entrepreneurial inspiration. "If that guy could make it with rice pudding," the thinking goes, "I can make it with anything." But it's not any old rice pudding. It's creamy new rice pudding, influenced by the creamy gelatos that Pete encountered in Italy. Pete envisioned the blend; Jemal Edwards, a pastry chef, created it. And a sign in the window defines it: "Finally, a rice pudding that doesn't suck."

Jemal has come up with 150 flavors. Pete has come up with names for all of them. On any day, you can ponder 21 of the named flavors. Among the favorites are Coast to Coast Cheesecake, Cinnamon Sling, Fluent in French Toast, and Sex Drugs and Rocky Road. If you think those puns are bad—or if you think they're good—consider the seasonal ones, such as summer's Pope Pina Colada II and It Takes Two to Peach Mango. Or winter's I Gotta the Panna Cotta. Or the holiday season's I'll Take Eggnog for $200 Alex.

The toppings range from whipped cream to espresso crumble, toasted pound cake, and oven-roasted fresh fruit. The sizes range from the 6-ounce Diva, which comes in four flavors, to the 80-ounce Moby, which is supposed to serve 10, but don't count on it. You make your choices after walking through an entrance shaped like a rice grain into a room shaped like a rice grain with a counter shaped like a rice grain. You can eat your pudding at a table shaped like a rice grain, while reading the signs, which are shaped like rice grains.

There was something about rice—but not at first about pudding. Pete imagined a place where he'd mix rice from everywhere with everything. Then he toured Florence, Rome, and Milan, got captivated by the gelatos, and pictured them as pudding. Then he pictured where the pudding would go. "I knew every element of the design long before the store was ever built," he says. He wanted color. He wanted excitement. He wanted things in the shape of rice. "I wanted to design a store so that people driving by in cars would have to stop and say: 'What the hell is that?'"

Jemal was able to translate Pete's pudding thoughts into puddings. As for the concept, Jemal acknowledges, he had some thoughts of his own: "I thought it was a bit wacky. But I knew there had been wackier ideas that had been successful. You never know. Especially in New York."

SCHNITZ

177 First Ave., New York, NY 10003
(646) 861-3923   schnitznyc.com

WORTH A STORY

Page six of *The Schnitz Chronicle* reports on the eruption of the deep fryer; page five reports on the impoundment of the Jeep; page four reports on the rainout of an outdoor market. You want to buy a sandwich just to help these people out.

Actually, though, they're doing swell. *The Schnitz Chronicle* is just a collection of blog posts about the challenges of doing swell. And it seems less odd that a restaurant would print a newspaper heralding its disasters when you find out that it's a schnitzel restaurant that doesn't serve traditional schnitzel.

There are lots of schnitzels, since schnitzel is basically flat, breaded, deep-fried meat, but the schnitzel that tends to come to mind, at least around here, is Wiener schnitzel. That name is German for "Vienna cutlet," and the cutlet is veal, which is just the kind of cutlet that you won't find at Schnitz. Schnitz was inspired by the schnitzel of Israel. The signature Schnitz schnitzels are made with chicken thighs. They come on a pretzel roll and are accompanied by a lemon wedge. The lemon, reports the *Chronicle*, is there for "rooting you on as you take each savory bite."

Among the chicken-thigh schnitzels are the Bamberg, which is topped with pickled cucumbers, daikon, ginger, shallots, and caramelized-onion Dijon mustard, and the Sweet Onion, which is topped with pickled cabbage, jicama, radish, cilantro, and roasted-beet tzatziki. There's also the Caesar, with black kale Caesar salad, fried egg, and Grana Padano, and the Mrs. Child, with Schnitz greens and celery-root remoulade. The Mrs. Child was so-named, says Yoni Erlich, one of Schnitz's founders, because the chef "thought that Julia Child would love the sandwich."

For those who don't love thighs, there are two pork schnitzels, one made with pork loin and the other with pork belly. There's also a shrimp schnitzel, with the cinematic name of Lt. Dan, and a butternut-squash-and-corn schnitzel, with the name of The Yonz. It's named for Yoni.

Yoni probably didn't open Schnitz to get a schnitzel named after him, but he probably did open it, at least in part, to get himself some schnitzel. He and his sister, Donna, grew up in New Jersey eating schnitzel made by their Israeli mother. It was hard to forget.

A few years ago Yoni and Donna were having drinks with their friend Allon Yosha, who also grew up eating Israeli schnitzel in New Jersey. "We had a lightbulb moment," Yoni says. "We wondered, is there a place to get schnitzel where you don't have to sit down at a restaurant?" They couldn't find one, so they considered the portable-schnitzel market theirs. Next they considered the artistic possibilities. "It's like a blank canvas, schnitzel," Yoni recalls thinking. "It could be turkey; it could be duck. Why can't it be the next falafel? Or even meatball?"

They proceeded to do the things you do to open a restaurant, with one difference: They recorded everything on a blog. "We soon realized we were in over our heads," Yoni says, "and we decided to use that to our advantage by documenting all our missteps and misfortune." They launched Schnitz in 2010 at Smorgasburg, the weekend food market in Brooklyn. The restaurant opened in 2014. In between, a restaurant called Schnitzel & Things came and went in Midtown. Yoni believes that it was a victim of uptown rent, which is why Schnitz is downtown.

At Schnitz, you can pick up a copy of *The Schnitz Chronicle* and read about the deep fryer, the Jeep, and the rain. But the most telling story may be the one by Donna about her brother, which concludes: ". . . thank you, Yoni! You are the most hard-working man in show-schnitz!"

SIGMUND'S PRETZELS

29 Avenue B, New York, NY 10009

(646) 410-0333   sigmundnyc.com

LIFE HAS TWISTS

A pretzel is not a doughnut. That's why there is no Plunkin' Pretzels. Yet a pretzel is by far the more versatile of the two. Try having a beer-brined, deboned chicken thigh roasted with parsley under the skin and stuffed into a jelly doughnut. Then say you wouldn't have swapped for a pretzel bun.

Versatility is the pretzel's ace in the hole. That's why Yuri Shutovsky turned his pretzel shop into a pretzel restaurant. At Sigmund's Pretzels, you can get not only soft pretzels with other foods on them, but also other foods with soft pretzels on, in, and around them.

"We thought that by opening a pretzel shop we were going to get the same traction as a doughnut shop, but we were wrong," Yuri says, since he's not given to spin. "Nobody comes to a store and buys a dozen pretzels. The product doesn't have the same emotional appeal as doughnuts." So in 2013 Sigmund's, the pretzel bakery, was reborn as Sigmund's, the gastropub. That meant the addition of beer, which is also more versatile than the doughnut, and the addition of pretzel lunches, brunches, dinners, and snacks to the original pretzels.

The original pretzels, besides the Classic pretzel, include the Truffle Cheddar pretzel, the Feta Olive pretzel, the Garlic Parsley pretzel, and the Cinnamon Raisin pretzel. They're not typically dunked, but they can be dipped, in dips including honey mustard, stone-ground mustard, and Nutella. Beyond those are snacks like the Antipretzel Platter, which has cheeses, pickles, and grilled pretzel bread. Beyond snacks are sandwiches, which, besides the Chicken Thigh, include a grilled cheese, a Reuben, and the Sigmund's Burger—which is topped with a fried egg—each on a pretzel bun. There are grilled sausages, including bratwurst, kielbasa, merguez, and chorizo, all served on pretzel rolls. For brunch, there's Pretzel Benedict, whose eggs are on pretzel bread. For dessert, there's Cinnamon Raisin Pretzel Bread Pudding with vanilla ice cream.

Yuri never dreamed of serving Cinnamon Raisin Pretzel Bread Pudding. He dreamed of food concepts far more revolutionary. They included a restaurant at which the tables would be lowered for dessert, and a Russian-Western restaurant that would feature what he called "Berlintzes." He did not pursue those particular dreams. Instead, he designed training software for a German bank in Moscow. It was his wife, Lina Kulchinsky, who first took the culinary career path, which is what led them to their comparatively practical pretzel concept.

Lina went to NYU to become a lawyer but switched to the Institute of Culinary Education and became a pastry chef. She worked for chefs like Jean Georges, and then for a catering company. Meanwhile, Yuri took a course called "How to Open a Restaurant." Though they both came from Russia and were living in America, they liked the idea of a shop that sold bread associated with Germany. Besides, soft pretzels are also associated with New York City, and not always in a good way. They knew they could improve on the wares of the typical cart.

They opened their pretzel bakery in 2009 and followed with a wholesale bakery in Brooklyn in 2010. They also added a little white pretzel cart that makes appearances at weddings, dispensing the food perhaps best qualified to symbolize tying the knot.

All of which leaves at least one question: Who is Sigmund? And Yuri answers it with his characteristic candor: "Sigmund is a name. We came up with the name because we were looking for a good name. And we thought that a person's name is a good name for a place."

S'MAC

345 E. 12th St., New York, NY 10003

(212) 358-7912   smacnyc.com

OUTSIDE THE BOX

There are those who ditch New York to live in a nice big house in New Hampshire and those who ditch a nice big house in New Hampshire to sell mac and cheese in New York. Sarita and Caesar Ekya are in the second group. In fact, they may constitute the second group.

As much as they loved the Granite State, they were drawn to the asphalt jungle. Once here, they had to justify their considerable loss of square footage. So they opened the city's first macaroni and cheese restaurant, which is on course to help them regain some of those lost square feet.

The restaurant is S'MAC, which stands for Sarita's Macaroni and Cheese. "He wanted me to be the face of the business," Sarita explains. "He said, 'You can be like Wendy.' I thought, no way was I gonna be up there with pigtails." But she liked the name S'MAC and it tested well in New Hampshire.

The S'MAC menu starts with the All-American, which has American and cheddar cheese, and the 4 Cheese, which has cheddar, Muenster, Gruyère, and pecorino. It moves on to the Cheeseburger, which adds ground beef to the All-American. From there it starts to get fancy. There's the Mediterranean, with goat cheese, sautéed spinach, kalamata olives, and roasted garlic; the Parisienne, with Brie, figs, roasted shitake mushrooms, and rosemary; and the Cajun, with cheddar, pepper jack, andouille sausage, green pepper, onions, celery, and garlic. The Cajun ingredient list is topped only by the Masala.

Your alternative is "Dare to Build Your Own?" Say yes, and you choose your own cheeses and "mix-ins." Besides those mentioned, the cheeses include blue, mozzarella, Manchego, Muenster, Parmesan, Swiss, and light cheddar. The dare is more about the mix-ins. They run from hot dogs to

broccoli, from figs to slab bacon, from tuna to cilantro to Buffalo sauce. "When we started the do-it-yourself menu, I was very scared," Sarita acknowledges. "Even though someone else creates it, the restaurant's gonna get the blame for it." Still, she took the chance, since taking chances had become a habit, pretty much from the time that she met Caesar.

Sarita, born in Nova Scotia, has a degree in mechanical engineering. Caesar, born in Kashmir, has a degree in electrical engineering. Caesar was engineering in Massachusetts and Sarita was engineering in New Hampshire when fate brought them together for a future in macaroni.

When they got married, they both traded their last names for the new one, Ekya, which in Sanskrit means "unity." Among what united them was New York, to which they drove regularly from their home in Manchester. Often they'd make the 500-mile round-trip in a day.

It was a matter of time before they quit their jobs and gave up their house. The turning point came at Peanut Butter & Co., the peanut-butter-sandwich restaurant. They pondered a place that would sell peanut butter, grilled cheese, and mac and cheese. Since the first two were taken, they honed in on the last. They left their house in 2005, following three colossal yard sales, which were essential to moving into a one-bedroom sublet. On the bright side, they'd be saving a fortune in gas. They opened S'MAC in June 2006, nine months after the turning point.

Other mac-and-cheese places popped up, but S'MAC held its ground. In 2012 it opened a Midtown branch three times the size of the original. The year before, it tried out a kiosk, but that didn't work out. "We know how to do brick and mortar," Sarita says, "so we're sticking to that." They also know how to do mac and cheese, though Sarita acknowledges that "you really can't go wrong if you use things in the right proportion."

"The only thing I've ever steered people away from is when they want to use just blue cheese. Even for macaroni, that's a lot of blue cheese."

Other location: 157 E. 33rd St., New York, NY 10016, (212) 683-3900

SNOWDAYS

241 E. 10th St., New York, NY 10003

(917) 402-6408   snowdaysnyc.com

CAN YOU DIG IT?

Having concluded that there was plenty of room for snow in New York, Tony Quach arranged to bring a load of it here from California. Not surprisingly, though, this snow is different. It comes in colors. It also comes with nuts and berries. And it comes with names like Yeti Tracks. This snow is snow cream, a cold dessert in the West that Tony is determined to make a cool dessert in the East. His determination can be observed at his shop, Snowdays/A Snow Cream Shavery, which appears to be the first major accumulation of snow cream in New York City.

Getting the drift of snow cream can be a challenge, since its name is reminiscent of several things it is not. It is not sno-cones, which are crunchy ice. It is not sno-balls, which are snowy ice. It is not Sno Balls, which are chocolate cake and marshmallow from Hostess. It is not even ice cream made with snow, which is also called snow cream. At Snowdays, snow cream is low-fat milk with heavy cream, frozen in blocks. The blocks are shaved into ribbons to create a cold comfort that is at once creamy, light, and fluffy, like snow with cream.

"I really feel like this is the new dessert wave," Tony says. "I see frozen yogurt going out, and snow cream coming in." Of course, if all the frozen yogurt left New York at once, we'd be left with Topeka. Still, snow cream at least seems to have the potential to compete.

At Snowdays it comes in flavors including New York cheesecake, roasted black sesame, sweet milk, green tea matcha, coconut, and Yeti Tracks, which is blueberry with Oreos. You can augment these with toppings and drizzles, at least if you're a competent augmenter. The toppings include Pocky sticks, mochi, grass jelly, red bean, almonds, peanuts, walnuts, Oreos,

Cap'n Crunch, Fruity Pebbles, Nilla Wafers, marshmallows, and granola. The drizzles include condensed milk, chocolate sauce, peanut butter sauce, and whipped cream.

If you're an incompetent augmenter, you might want to choose from the Combos, which include the Yeti Food, which is Yeti Tracks snow cream with bananas, sugar cones, and blueberry purée, and the Almond Joy, coconut snow cream with almonds, M&Ms, and salted caramel sauce.

All of this was precipitated in Los Angeles, where Tony discovered snow cream while on leave from Manhattan. He'd been a paralegal here and was a green-energy consultant there. When he tasted the cream, he says, "I thought, 'I need to bring this back to New York.'" He adopted ideas of Western cream spots with names like SweetSnow and Blockheads, but he found those places just a little too bound to their Asian roots. "It was all green tea, red bean, and sweet milk," he says. "That's OK, but I wanted to put a little more New York attitude in it." That explains the Yeti Tracks and the New York cheesecake, along with the photos of city street scenes on the walls. It also explains the decks of cards: "I wanted this to be a place where people hang out. I'm not trying to franchise this out. I'm serving the neighborhood."

Tony created the recipes and tested his creams at several locations, with the help of his Brooklynite friend Eric Nieves. The creams passed their tests, so he looked for a spot, aiming at the East Village. He opened the store in 2014. Eric is the snow operations manager.

The first day was "five hours of mayhem." People couldn't get enough of the stuff. People also couldn't get exactly what the stuff was. They still can't. "They call it shaved cream," Tony says. "They call it shaved ice. They call it shaved ice cream. They call it everything but snow cream."

SOCKERBIT

89 Christopher St., New York, NY 10014

(212) 206-8170   sockerbit.com

SCOOPING SURA SKALLAR

If you don't know your bumlingar jordgubb from your rabarberbitar, you might start your learning process by popping some hallonbatar. After all, there's nothing like a raspberry boat. It's not easy to find, or at least it wasn't, until it sailed into town and docked at Sockerbit.

Raspberry boats are little red candies that are beloved in Sweden, which is why they go by the name of hallonbatar. Bumlingar jordgubb are strawberry candies. Rabarberbitar are licorice candies. Sockerbit is a marshmallow that's the namesake of the store where you bag them.

The store is billed as "Sweet & Swedish" since those words alliterate, but it's really a kaleidoscope of confections from Scandinavia. The centerpiece is a wall of bins that showcase 130 or so candies classified as sweet, sour, licorice, hard, chocolate, and marshmallow. You look at the pretty colors, you ponder the alien names, and you read the English descriptions if you are risk-averse. You pick up a bag and a scoop, and dump what you want into the bag. You get as much or as little as you want for the same price per pound.

Freedom and equality are attractions, but the biggest one is the candy, says the owner of Sockerbit, Stefan Ernberg. He has lived abroad a lot, he says, and when Swedes like him do that, they "realize how good the candy is that we have at home. We wanted to share that."

In the sweet category, along with hallonbatar, they share another classic: gelehallon, which are sugar-encrusted raspberry drops. Also rabarberbitar, which, more specifically, are rhubarb licorice with lemon filling, and fruxo, which are "yummy chewy mini fruit gummies." Sour selections include sura persikobitar, "a sweet creamy peachy interior with a sour exterior."

Licorice choices include salta salmiak pastiller, "crazy salty licorice. Only for the brave." Hard candies include the bumlinger jordgubb, strawberry orbs "meant to be enjoyed slowly."

Some names reveal more than others; you can more or less crack monikers like chokobananer, yoghurt kokocluster, and tutti frutti ovaler. Some candies reveal more than others; you don't necessarily need to know that the little green jelly frogs are called grona grodor. In the end, though, it's all about taste: Scandinavian candies are just more vivid than most, Stefan promises. "People are surprised at how much flavor there is in the candy," he says. "It's not like, 'Oh, what am I eating? It says here it's pineapple. OK. It's pineapple.'"

In his homeland, of course, they're used to the flavor. They buy this stuff in supermarkets. But here, he knew, Scandinavian candy would be something special. His wife, Florencia Baras, agreed, even though she's from Argentina. In 2009 they embarked on what Stefan calls "the Sockerbit project." They found their location and their inspiration: the chewy little white marshmallow whose name means "sugar cube" in Swedish. Along with its name, it lent its look: Everything in the store is marshmallow-white. Your eyes go straight to the candy, if only for relief.

They have other strategies. The couple keep the candy types mingled, so that whatever you happen to be looking for, you'll be looking at something else. They also kept the foreign names. "We wanted to have that exotic feeling," Stefan says. "We make it a little difficult for people, so they'll interact." It all seems to work. Sockerbit opened in 2011, and three years later it opened a store in Los Angeles. That one looks like a marshmallow, too. "People remember us," Stefan says. "Maybe they won't remember the name Sockerbit, but they will remember that white candy store."

STICKY'S FINGER JOINT

31 W. Eighth St., New York, NY 10011
(212) 777-7131   stickysfingerjoint.com

GLITTERING ACHIEVEMENT

Sticky is a robot. As such, he's not generally hungry. Yet he's portrayed grasping a strip of chicken and a bottle of dipping sauce. Perhaps he's transmitting the message that the food at his namesake restaurant is so tasty that it can foster an appetite even in squat red automatons. Either way, that's the point. Sticky's set out to take a fast-food staple and transform it into a fast-casual star. It succeeded. Sticky's Finger Joint has made gourmet food of chicken fingers—and a name for itself, for better or for worse, on national TV.

Fingers, of course, are everywhere. They're famously at burger chains and fried-chicken chains, and less famously at exclusively finger chains. The latter include Guthrie's Golden Fried Chicken Fingers and Raising Cane's Chicken Fingers, but neither of those has a place in New York. Typically, however, a finger is a finger. It's a ribbon of fried chicken that you dunk in a puddle. You can usually choose among quantities and combos, but not among seasonings and sauces. Sticky's made a simple thing complicated. That's why it belongs in New York.

The Sticky's "laboratory" has cooked up several dozen fingers and sauces. The fingers rotate; the sauces remain stationary. Most of the fingers and sauces bear vibrant names and descriptions and, combined with the place's robotic decor, evoke a deep-fried Neverland.

Consider the Bada Bing. It's "Chicken parm in finger form! Marinara buttermilk brined, breaded in Italian panko breading, stuffed with low-moisture mozzarella and parmesan and then topped with marinara, tomato aioli, fried basil and BadaBing Glitter. Bada Boom!!!" Consider the Salted Caramel: "We are in cahoots with the Tooth Fairy. Buttermilk brined, coated in crunchy crushed pretzel, smothered in salted caramel, garnished with pretzel sticks and pretzel glitter. Delicious, sticky and sure to please."

Other fingers include the Wasabi (with "wasabi glitterbang"), the Fiesta (with Fiesta glitter), and the Vampire Killer ("enough garlic to ward off all bloodsuckers"). There are also the self-evident Buffalo Balsamic Maple, General Sticky Tso, and Fire Flame Curry (with coconut glitter).

On top of this, you can add sauces, which you pick from a list of 15. They begin mildly, with Sticky's Sauce ("North Alabama barbecue with an NYC kick"). After Buttermilk Baby Ranch they heat up with stuff like Sriracha Ranch and Chocolate Chipotle BBQ. There's Thai Sweet Chili Sauce, Mango Death Sauce, and Wasabi Aoli, which has wasabi glitter, rather than wasabi glitterbang. There are a couple more aiolis, a couple of mustards, and balsamic ketchup. Choose boldly, and you'll eat something that tastes like nothing you've ever eaten.

That was what the creator, Paul Abrahamian, sought to create. A "serial entrepreneur," he always meant to get his hands on fingers. "I literally grew up on chicken fingers," he says. "I must have had chicken fingers three or four times a week." No wonder he wanted them glittered and banged.

His project before Sticky's was a tech start-up in China. "Things weren't working out so well, so I turned to my love of food. I looked at the market and saw that there really wasn't an option for fast-casual chicken." A lesser man might have taken that as a warning.

He teamed up with Jonathan Sherman, whose father had worked for the Bojangles' chicken chain. They picked a location and a robot. Then Paul pitched TV—and Sticky's ended up as an episode of a Food Network series called *3 Days to Open with Bobby Flay.* It was called "A Sticky Situation," and it was not what you'd call flattering. It was also, according to Paul, not what you'd call factual. "Reality TV is all about humiliation and redemption," he says. Besides, Sticky's has lasted for more than three years. *3 Days* lasted six episodes.

Other location: 484 Third Ave., New York, NY 10016, (646) 490-5856

TREAT HOUSE

452 Amsterdam Ave., New York, NY 10024

(212) 799-7779   treathouse.com

BEYOND MEMORY

Here's your chance to be an adult who feels like a child who's eating a snack for a child that's made for an adult.

The chance was made possible by a couple of adults and a couple of children.

Treat House is a restaurant devoted to a reinvention of the timeless snack most commonly known as Rice Krispies Treats. Such treats are blocks of toasted-rice breakfast cereal mixed with melted marshmallow and butter or margarine. This is a place devoted to that.

Since "Treat House" sounds like "tree house," the owners installed a nook at the back of the store that looks like it belongs on a branch. It has a blackboard, pennants, and a table with tree-stump seats. You can sneak your treats back there and hardly anyone will see. But, of course, these are not the treats that you ate as a child on the branch of a tree. These are treats dressed up to be sold on the Upper West Side of New York. They are made by a pastry chef, and they have ingredients like chocolate ganache, almond bark, blueberry powder, and candied lemon rind.

The treats come in flavors like Cranberry Orange, Maple Pecan, Chocolate Pretzel, Oreo, and Birthday Cake. Each one is a 1½-inch cube, and each one wears a hat. Chocolate Peanut Butter, for instance, is topped with a chunk of peanut-butter cup. Bubble Gum is crowned with a wad of Dubble Bubble. Thus the treats are suitable for dinner parties and wedding receptions. This explains why one costs as much as a small box of Rice Krispies. These treats are the epicurean version of the ones you can buy at the gas mart. Malitta and Mildred would be tickled, if perhaps mystified.

Mildred Day and Malitta Jensen were the inventors of Rice Krispies Treats. They invented them in 1939, in the kitchens of Kellogg's. Their treats were called Marshmallow Squares, but their recipe hasn't changed much except for losing their dash of vanilla. Rice Krispies were 11 years old at the time. Since then, countless people have meddled with the treats in count-less ways. Kellogg's itself started packaging them in 1995. Still, nothing has quite topped the taste of the warm stringy mass you scrape out of your pot, if you can. Chris Russell saw this as a challenge.

Chris is a veteran New York City restaurateur. He is also a father, which was pivotal to the building of Treat House. In 2011 his sons Daniel and Eli wanted to raise money for children in Africa. Maybe because they knew Dad could cook, they decided to sell treats. Chris, with the help of the boys and his wife, Jennifer, came up with three flavors: Chocolate Mint, Butterscotch Sprinkle, and Raspberry Chocolate. They sold out in two hours. "A couple of weeks later," Chris says, "it dawned on my wife and me that there were so many potential flavor combinations."

They enlisted the help of a pastry chef, Wendy Israel. The treat team spent two years refining treat-making techniques. "We learned early on," Chris says, "that if you just add ingredients to crisp rice cereal, you get soggy crisp rice cereal, and nobody wants that." Nevertheless, Chris says, his treats can take acclimation. "They're not traditional Rice Krispies Treats," he says. They're also not made with Rice Krispies. "We pack them denser than you would at home. So sometimes people's expectations of what it should taste like are different from what it does taste like."

He isn't worried, though. He was once the chef for the rarefied restaurant Moomba, and while a treat place is different, in a way, he says, it's the same: "If you want a two-dollar brick of Rice Krispies, you go to the deli. If you want something a little more sophisticated, you come here."

TUCK SHOP

68 E. First St., New York, NY 10003

(212) 979-5200   tuckshopnyc.com

HUMBLE PIE

If you want a typical Australian meat pie, go to a gas station in Australia. If you want an authentic Australian meat pie, go to Tuck Shop in New York. A tuck shop, after all, is a food shop, and a meat pie is a food, though the ones at those gas stations leave some room for debate. Originally a hand-made food, the pies now are often factory-made foods, sold under dubiously evocative brand names like Four'N Twenty. They are found not only at gas stations but also at Aussie sporting events, where instead of yelling "Hot dogs!" the vendors yell "Hot pies!"

The founders of Tuck Shop wanted to bring back the old-time hot pies, and they decided to do it in New York, where there are no Australian gas stations. The store opened in 2005 and has since been enticing Americans to try its pies, which it has labeled "The Great Aussie Bite."

It has the Traditional Meat Pie, in which "meat" means ground beef, and the Thai Chook Curry Pie, in which "chook" means chicken. It has the Guinness Steak and Mushroom Pie, the Lamb Shank and Vegetable Pie, the BBQ Pork Pie, and for staunch Americans, the Chicken Pot Pie. If you want meat pies without meat, there's the Mac 'N' Cheese Pie, along with the Vegetarian Chili Pie and the Vegetable Lentil Pie. There are also sides of roasted Brussels sprouts and kale salad for the health-conscious, and a side of Mash & Gravy for the mash-and-gravy-conscious.

You can eat walking, since these pies are built for that, but the shop welcomes you to dine in. It has a counter, a couple of tables, and many authentic Australian artifacts. These include a boomerang, a cricket bat, a koala tin, blow-up kangaroos, old Cheezels boxes, and a copy of AC/DC's *Back in Black*. It also has the table on which the pies are made, so you can

watch as a boulder of dough is turned into your lunch. This impressed an Aussie customer named Peter Freudenberger, who told me: "In eighteen years in Australia I never saw a pie being made—just like you never see a hot dog being made here."

"In Australia," Peter explained, "eating meat pies is something you do very casually. . . . It's not a fine dining thing. This place replicates the experience, but you get good food. . . . There are all those corner delis that sell pizza and pasta. It's like going from that to a place that sells real pizza and pasta."

The opportunity for this was set in motion over a decade ago, when an Australian named Lincoln Davies came to America. "I came here with the idea of a two-week holiday," he says. Instead, he saw that America was short on meat pies and he made it his mission to help us out. He got his friend Niall Grant to help, too, and in a few years they launched the store. A few years later they opened a store on St. Mark's Place. They followed that with one at the Chelsea Market, which is still thriving. The St. Mark's shop is gone, but it taught them about challenges.

Among their challenges has been the New York City debut of Pie Face, the Australian meat-pie chain that paints faces on its pies. It opened its first city store in 2012 and got up to eight. But in late 2014 it closed seven of those eight. Another challenge has been Dub Pies, which opened in the West Village in 2013—but closed that branch in 2014. In any case, Niall takes an enterprising view of competitors. "They're educating the marketplace," he says. At least they were.

There's still a lot to learn, Niall says, and now he's teaching alone, since Lincoln decided that he'd had his fill of pies. "Meat pie," Niall says, "doesn't sound very sexy to the American ear. People want pumpkin pie, pecan pie, pizza pie. I'm hoping to change that, one person at a time."

Other location: Chelsea Market, 75 Ninth Ave., New York, NY 10011, (212) 255-2021

DON'T HAVE A COW

Sophia Brittan named her shop Victory Garden for a couple of reasons, but not for what have proved to be her two great victories: getting people to learn that there is ice cream at a place called Victory Garden, and getting people to learn to eat ice cream made with goat milk.

Sophia believes that goat milk is better for you than cow milk, but she understands that the primary job of ice cream is to be nummy. While she can talk digestibility and human compatibility, she knows her selling points: "It's a delicious dessert. It's not something weird." That said, you might still find it weird since, in her deviation from ice-cream conventions, Sophia doesn't stop at the milk. Once you get past the goat, you encounter things like lavender, thyme, and turmeric. Fortunately, at that point, you might be ready for them.

The ice cream—or "soft serve," as Sophia alternately calls it since, by definition, it's not exactly ice cream—was inspired by dondurma, which is Turkish ice cream, which is made with salep, an orchid-root flour, and mastic, a tree resin, which also aren't weird. At Victory Garden, you're less likely to find Chocolate than you are to find Chocolate Cardamom, Chocolate Rosemary, or Chocolate Mastic, just as you're less likely to find Vanilla than you are to find Saffron Vanilla, Orange Blossom Vanilla, or Mexican Vanilla with agave. You might also find Violet, Honey Lavender, Rose Petal, Blood Orange Clove, Ethiopian Coffee, and Jasmine Green Tea. You might even find The Healing Powers of India, which is made with carrots, turmeric, ginger, and nigella seeds. Even so, the bestseller is Salted Caramel.

Sophia is partial to combinations like Pistachios, Sour Cherries and Mastic, since she's partial to mastic (which is in abundance at a store called

Mastihashop). At home, she has it in everything from her water to her soap and shampoo. At her shop, you can get it in mastic chewing gum. As for the goat milk, besides the soft serve, it turns up in sandwiches, salads, rolls, and cheesecake, not to mention soap, hand lotion, and lip balm. But the soft serve is the star, because it can show off all those flavors, which inspired Sophia at least as much as the milk.

She grew up in Connecticut with a family that loved food and travel. She went to Georgetown University, where she majored in Middle East studies. Through Georgetown, she studied in the Dominican Republic and in Egypt, after which she studied in Lebanon, where she found her inspiration. She came to New York and went to the French Culinary Institute. She launched *Kitchen Caravan*, an online cooking show, with her friend Emma Piper-Burket, and met a farmer who, she says, "made really good goat-milk yogurt." At first, she thought of a goat-milk yogurt shop, but she thought again. She went to Turkey, came back, and developed her own version of dondurma, then opened Victory Garden in 2011. She named it for the gardens that helped supply food during the World Wars—and for herself. Sophia is her middle name. Victoria is her first.

Some people, she says, come in because they've never had goat-milk ice cream. Other people come in especially because they have. "So many Jamaicans come in and say, 'My grandmother had a goat, and I had that milk warm,'" Sophia says. She'll do what she can to prove it's not weird.

The main thing she has to do is explain what goat milk is not: "A lot of people seem to think goat milk comes out in the form of cheese. They picture something sweet being made with goat cheese. They say, 'I've never had goat-cheese ice cream.' I say, 'I haven't either.'"

WAFELS & DINGES

15 Avenue B, New York, NY 10009

(212) 510-7114   wafelsanddinges.com

NO LOG CABIN

Wafels and dinges may sound like two foods, whether or not you can pronounce them, until you learn that dinges isn't a food—which makes this a wafel cafe. It's a wafel cafe from a wafel truck from a man who comes from Belgium. In Flemish, which people speak in Belgium, wafel means waffle, and dinges, which is pronounced "ding-ess," means whatsis or whosis, as in: "I was out looking for waffles when I saw that guy dinges."

At Wafels & Dinges, dinges refers to the things you can have on the waffles, which range from the customary maple syrup to the less customary barbecued pork. "America knows two kinds of waffles," says Thomas DeGeest, the man from Belgium, "the diner waffle and the Eggo waffle." He doesn't waffle.

Wafels & Dinges spotlights two kinds of waffles, but not the aforementioned two. They are the Brussels, which is "lite 'n crispy" and the Liège, which is "soft 'n chewy." You can turn either waffle into a meal, or a dessert, or a dessert that's a meal, by topping it with the appropriate dinges.

If you lean toward customary, you might choose from—besides maple syrup—butter, sugar, bananas, strawberries, walnuts, Nutella, dulce de leche, whipped cream, ice cream, chocolate fudge, and spekuloos spread, a gingery topping named for a Belgian cookie. If you lean toward uncustomary, your choice might be the barbecued pork, the Bauerenschinken ham with raclette cheese and scallions, or the bacon and syrup. Or perhaps you'd prefer the potato waffle with sour cream and prune syrup, or the corn waffle with chili, sour cream, and cilantro. Beyond uncustomary, there are choices like the Oh Oh Serrano, a "flavor fest on a grilled Brussels wafel with serrano ham, asiago cheese & fig spread," and the 2nd Street Salmon

Special, also a Brussels wafel, this time with smoked salmon, capers, red onion, and lemon-dill sour cream.

Some of those choices are too complicated for the food truck, which was one of the reasons that Thomas decided to open a cafe. Another was to provide the Americans who know two waffles with the opportunity to find some others, in a place that won't roll away. Still, that wasn't his first goal. His first goal was to be something other than a management consultant for IBM. He needed a change, and he thought of waffles. Not that he'd ever made waffles, but he had eaten them. That seemed like enough to justify buying a used food truck.

It was a 1968 Chevy, and this was 2007. It had its share of problems before it stopped running at all. "We couldn't find parts," Thomas recalls, "so we towed it around behind my car with a rope. We'd turn a corner and pedestrians wouldn't realize the two were together, and they'd try to walk between them." This landed Thomas in court before a judge with a soft spot for waffles. The judge dismissed the case, but the Chevy was retired. Thomas got a new truck, which led to the current fleet of two trucks and five carts, all of which have names and are referred to as persons.

Thomas was among the pioneers of the latter-day food truck, and his contributions have been recognized and rewarded. Assorted notable sources have designated his trucks the "Most Popular," the "Most Influential," and among the "25 Most Fantastic." As a wheel on wheels, he could afford to open a place that stayed put, which he did in 2013. It's a sparkling space with homey accents like old waffle irons. It plays with its native tongue in signs that say things like "de sweet wafels" and "de orderin' happens dat-a-way."

But then, you want a waffle guy who's light about waffles—not to mention honest, which Thomas also is. "My favorite," he says, "is the Brussels with powdered sugar. I don't need strawberries, bananas, chocolate, or peanut butter. I like to taste the waffle."

YONAH SCHIMMEL KNISH BAKERY

137 E. Houston St., New York, NY 10002
(212) 477-2858   knishery.com

ONE-CENTURY WONDER

The single-food restaurant, of course, is nothing new, unless you don't consider 105 to be old. Either way, it's old enough to make Yonah Schimmel the great-grandpa of the single-food restaurant in New York City. The Yonah Schimmel Knish Bakery actually dates back to the 19th century, when it began as a pushcart on Coney Island. The pushcart moved to the Lower East Side, then graduated to a store, which crossed the street to its current location in 1910. It hasn't changed since.

Or so it seems. Besides being one of the oldest stores in New York, it's one of the oldest-looking stores in New York. The outside looks merely aged, but the inside could make it into *Guinness World Records* in the category of Most Layers of Red and White Paint. Ensconced in red and white, you can sit at a red-and-white table and have a knish that's just like the ones Yonah sold from his cart, or you can be adventurous and have a knish that's nothing like the ones Yonah sold from his cart, and that nevertheless seems somehow authentic.

When you see a knish at all these days, it's often square and fried, but a traditional knish is round and baked, and that's the one you get at Yonah's. It's a stuffed dumpling, like pierogi, ravioli, and empanadas, but it's not like any of those. It's thin-skinned and overstuffed. Every one of the savory knishes is stuffed with potato. The potato knish has just potato; the kasha knish ("the world's second favorite") has kasha and potato. After that, the knishes mostly hold less tradition but, for a lot of people in the 21st century, more appeal. There's a spinach knish, a broccoli knish, and a

red-cabbage knish ("sweet, sharp & tangy"). There's a mushroom knish, a mixed-vegetable knish, and a sweet-potato knish ("a down South favorite"). And every day there's a special knish that Yonah could not have imagined.

Among them are the potato-and-cheddar knish, the jalapeño-and-cheddar knish, the potato-and-mozzarella knish, the jalapeño-and-mozzarella knish, the toasted-garlic-and-onion knish, the red-pepper-and-fried-onion knish, and, to save you another stop, the pizza knish. On top of that, there are sweet knishes in apple-cheese, cherry-cheese, blueberry-cheese, chocolate-cheese, plain-cheese, and apple strudel. All of the knishes are still hand-made, sent up in a dumbwaiter, and displayed in a glass counter that Yonah might have built.

And yet knishes weren't Yonah's first choice. He was a scribe, maybe a rabbi, says Ellen Anistratov, who runs the store with her father, Alex Volfman. "What he wanted was to teach people spirituality," she says. "But people were getting their means together. They didn't have money for spirituality." That's why Yonah's wife baked knishes for Yonah to sell from a pushcart, and it's why Ellen believes that Yonah's spirituality lives on in the store. "This is a very soothing food," she says. "People like to be here. They connect to the energy of the store. They connect to something higher."

How knishes themselves got started nobody really knows. It's likely that, in some form, they go back several centuries. But they got started in New York by the Jewish immigrants on the Lower East Side. A century ago, there were many knish places there. Now there's Yonah Schimmel.

Ellen at least partly credits the filling-to-shell ratio. "Yonah Schimmel's are very little dough and a lot of stuffing," she says. Alex further credits the long-standing wisdom to leave them alone. They've lasted, he says, "because we make them the same like a hundred years ago."

MORE ONE-FOOD WONDERS

ARTICHOKE BASILLE'S PIZZA, 114 10th Ave., New York, NY 10011, (212) 792-9200; 111 MacDougal St., New York, NY 10012, (646) 278-6100; 328 E. 14th St., New York, NY 10012, (212) 228-2004; artichokepizza.com
New York has a lot of pizza, but not a lot of it is green. That begins to explain the success of Artichoke Pizza. It sells a pistachio-green pie whose secret sauce is rich in artichokes and whose flavor has conjured up everything from mayonnaise to cream-of-artichoke soup. The pie was invented by Francis Garcia as an appetizer for his mother's restaurant, Basille's, which was on Staten Island. When he saw the reaction, he was convinced that the pie could stand on its own. He and his cousin Sal Basille opened Artichoke Basille's in 2008.

It sells some other pies, but the star is still the thistle. It led not only to other branches, but considerably beyond. The cousins opened Chubby Mary's, an Italian hero spot; Led Zeppole, a carnival-food spot; and This Little Piggy Had Roast Beef, a roast-beef-sandwich spot. Sadly, those have all closed. Artichoke Pizza, on the other hand, still has its three stores in Manhattan. It also has one each at La Guardia Airport and Resorts World in Queens, and in Berkeley, California. The cousins, as always, are searching for their next artichoke.

BEARD PAPA'S FRESH'N NATURAL CREAM PUFFS, 2167 Broadway, New York, NY 10024; (212) 799-3770; muginohointl.com
A cream puff is much like a bridal couple: Its members should be kept separate until it's time for them to be joined. That's a tenet of Beard Papa's, where you pick a shell and a filling and before your eyes the two are married. After which, they are consumed.

This store is the sole New York link in the Japanese chain, which began in Osaka in 1999. It's duly treasured by the New Yorkers who are stuck on its puffs. "We have a real loyal following," says Heirim Yoon, the chain's marketing director. "It's almost like a cult." The shells include the Paris Brest, which itself is portrayed as representing the marriage of a doughnut and a churro. The fillings include vanilla, chocolate, strawberry, banana, green tea, and espresso. Among the store favorites is the Dulce De Leche, a shell filled with cream and caramel.

The store opened in 2004. It's now one of 350—and some credit must go to Papa. He's a cartoon in white whiskers and a cap, supposedly modeled after an uncle of the founder. "He had a puffy beard," Heirim says. "He was sort of a cross between Santa Claus and Popeye."

CROISSANTERIA, 68 Avenue A, New York, NY 10009; (212) 466-2860; croissanterianyc.com

As long as all the other pastries were getting homes of their own, Selmo Ribeiro and David Simon figured they'd give one to the croissant. It's not a cafe with only croissants, but it's a cafe with enough croissants and enough stuff on croissants to merit the name of Croissanteria.

It has almond croissants, chocolate croissants, and almond-and-chocolate croissants, along with apricot croissants and just plain Croissanteria croissants. It has a peanut-butter-and-jelly croissant, a Nutella-and-banana croissant, a grilled-cheese croissant, and seven more-complex croissants. These include the French Ham, with Gruyère, sliced ham, Dijonaise sauce, and butter; the Italian Tuna, with tuna, red onion, celery, arugula, and tomato; and the Prosciutto di Parma, with buffalo mozzarella, sliced prosciutto, tomato, basil, extra-virgin olive oil, and cracked pepper.

David once worked at an upstate smokehouse owned by his father. Selmo founded the Nah Nah Bah cafe in Lagos, Portugal. But both loved New York and both believed in oneness: "If you're in New York," Selmo says, "the more niche you go in what you offer, the better you can make it."

DOUGH LOCO, 24 E. 97th St., New York, NY 10029; (212) 410-6297; doughloco.com

Corey Cova was into loco before he was into dough. He liked to whip up the unexpected with whatever was available. It's how he whipped up the breakfast sandwich at the nearby Earl's Beer & Cheese: cheddar, pork belly, kimchi, and fried egg on sourdough. At Dough Loco, the signature doughnut is the Maple Miso, which is glazed with maple syrup and miso paste. Another favorite is the Blueberry Lime, with glazes of blueberry-rosemary and lime. Other choices include the Green Apple Wasabi and the Banana Curry Dulce de Leche.

Corey, a CIA graduate, started out cooking on a US Navy submarine, which, he says, got him used to working in small spaces. He was thus a good fit for Earl's, from which he went to ABV wine bar. Both spots are owned by Michael Cesari, who now also owns Dough Loco. At ABV Corey developed his "highbrow-lowbrow" motif, which led to creations like Spam-Octopus Salad and the Foie-Gras Fluffernutter. He brought the concept to doughnuts in 2013. In 2015 he moved on to Lord Hamm's, whose specialty is gigantic sandwiches.

ED'S LOBSTER BAR, 222 Lafayette St., New York, NY 10012, (212) 343-3236; Gansevoort Market, 52 Gansevoort St., New York, NY 10014, (646) 943-1112; lobsterbarnyc.com

It isn't easy to get your claws on a menu that offers lobster in as many ways as Ed's. That's why Ed created his menu. Ed McFarland thought that the city needed a reminder that lobsters can do a lot more than get on a roll, whether or not the lobsters agreed.

Along with its lobster roll, Ed's has a pound-and-a-half steamed or grilled lobster and a broiled pound-and-a-half lobster with bread crumbs and garlic. But it also has a lobster burger, lobster ravioli, lobster pot pie, and a lobster galette, which is a lobster potato cake. On Wednesdays it has lobster meatballs over linguine, and on occasion it has specials like lobster farfalle. It doesn't have a lot of room; most diners sit at the white marble counter. But that counter's often packed, which suggests that Ed was correct in his thinking.

The main request he gets is for shelling lessons. "That's the one thing people don't know—how to get the meat out of a lobster," he says. Still, he supplies no bibs: "I'm very anti-bib. It kind of cheapens the experience. And you're gonna get it on you, no matter what."

EILEEN'S SPECIAL CHEESECAKE, 17 Cleveland Place, New York, NY 10012; (212) 966-5585; eileenscheesecake.com
When Eileen Avezzano says that her secret ingredient is love, you are uncharacteristically inclined to believe it. After all, it takes something special to make a tiny shop a giant among purveyors of the city's most famous cake, and whatever it is, Eileen's has it.

It has it in 40 flavors, that being one for each of its years, the latest (for 2015) being salted caramel. Among the others, besides the fruit-topped, are peanut butter, pumpkin, chocolate raspberry, mango, caramel pecan, rocky road, cookies-n-cream, and Bailey's Irish Coffee.

The original recipe was Eileen's mother's. A deli owner nudged Eileen into following it after her mother died. Eileen made the cakes in her apartment, and the owner sold them in his deli. She opened her shop on Cleveland Place because it was then "a ghost town"—meaning cheap rent.

Since then, her cakes have consistently made the lists of the city's best. But she still has just the original store, and she is still usually in it. "Cheesecake has given me everything I could possibly want," she says. "There's no reason to leave here. It's a happy corner."

FAT WITCH BAKERY, Chelsea Market, 75 Ninth Avenue, New York, NY 10011; (212) 807-1335; fatwitch.com
People who shop here actually refer to brownies as witches, which is a testament to Patricia and a tribute to Pamela. When both women were Wall

Street traders, Patricia baked brownies and Pamela ate them. Others ate them, too. But Pamela had an indelible trait.

"She had a laugh just like a witch," Patricia Helding says. "She had a cackle. And she would just dive into the brownies. I'd say, 'Pamela, be careful; you're gonna turn into a fat witch.'" When Patricia traded Wall Street for a brownie shop, at least she left with a brand name.

The name worked: Fat Witch opened in 1998, and Patricia is still baking nothing but witches. They come in varieties including double chocolate, caramel, and cinnamon cappuccino, with monthly specials like pecan shortbread, lavender, and whiskey ("the Drunken Witch").

There are big witches and baby witches, and along with one for yourself you can get lots for others, in prepackaged boxes, bags, and tins. Or you can get lots for yourself. Patricia's not making any promises, but she does happen to mention that Pamela is still skinny.

GEM SPA, 131 Second Ave., New York, NY 10003; (212) 995-1866
Gem Spa is a newsstand, which, along with the news, has candy, toys, sunglasses, hats, sundries, and a Zoltar machine. But its reputation is built on a drink, which is mixed at the checkout counter and modestly described on the awning: "New York's Best Egg Cream." An egg cream is made by mixing chocolate syrup, milk, and seltzer. The drink is believed to have first been mixed on the Lower East Side. It was once available in lots of places, including newsstands. It may or may not have originally been made with egg and cream.

The egg cream dates to at least the turn of the last century. Gem Spa dates to at least 1927. The stand has had several owners, and they've reportedly passed down their recipe. Gem became the last egg-cream newsstand standing. Now it's an attraction.

It makes four flavors of egg cream, though to connoisseurs only chocolate counts. The drinks are mixed at a tiny soda fountain. It's up to the drinker, of course, whether Gem Spa actually mixes New York's best. Still, to be safe, the owner asks people not to photograph the mixing.

GO! GO! CURRY!, 144 W. 19th St., New York, NY 10011, (212) 255-4555; 231 Thompson St., New York, NY 10012, (212) 505-2555; 273 W. 38th St., New York, NY 10018, (212) 730-5555; 12 John St., New York, NY 10038, (212) 406-5555; gogocurryusa-ny.com

Maybe it makes sense that an Indian food that came to the Japanese from the British would arrive in America with a baseball theme and a gorilla. Maybe not. But it's what happened. The food, in this case, came with Go! Go! Curry!, the place where your curry fix comes with a fixation.

Japan's version of curry is a veritable national dish. Go! Go! Curry! is a Japanese chain that arrived here in 2007. Along with its food, it brought its adulation of Hideki Matsui, the Japanese ballplayer who played for the Yomiuri Giants and, at the time, for the New York Yankees.

In Japan, Matsui's number was 55, which in Japanese is pronounced "go go"—thus the name. Thus also the 55-minute cooking processes, the 5/5 grand opening, and the 10:55-to-9:55 store hours, not to mention the joints' phone numbers. As for the food, the "stadiums" serve their thick, dark sauce over rice, accompanied by things like a fried chicken cutlet or a fried pork cutlet. The specials include the Home Run. The sizes are Walk, Single, Double, and Triple. The gorilla is the store mascot, which somehow begins to makes sense.

GRAND CENTRAL OYSTER BAR & RESTAURANT, Grand Central Terminal, New York, NY 10017; (212) 490-6650; oysterbarny.com

There are other places where you can eat oysters in New York, but no other places where you can eat them under Guastavino-tile ceilings. The Grand Central Oyster Bar & Restaurant is as grand a place as you'll find for indulging in Beavertails, Blue Diamonds, and Blackberry Points. It is grand because it was built as part of Grand Central Terminal, and they just don't build train stations or oyster bars the way they did in 1913. Its sprawling space is topped with five vaults of herringbone tiles, which were cleaned up to look like new in 2014.

You can have oysters in the dining room. You can have oysters at horseshoe counters. You can have oysters at the actual 22-seat bar. Every day you can choose from around 30 different oysters. Some days you can dine among close to 400 people.

It's a lucky thing. In the '70s the Oyster Bar was terminal, but it was rescued by the legendary restaurateur Jerry Brody. Two decades later it was ravaged by fire, and Brody rescued it again. So when you come, take a look at his portrait, when you're not looking at the ceiling.

KOSSAR'S BIALYS, 367 Grand St., New York, NY 10002; (212) 473-4810; kossarsbialys.com

In a way, the bialy is the rich man's bagel. It has nourishment in the middle, where a bagel has a hole. Apparently, that wasn't enough to prevent its receding from common usage to the point where it had only one store devoted to it in all of New York City. Yet in 2013 it had enough life in it to inspire three guys to try giving the old roll a new spin. Evan Giniger, Marc Halprin, and David Zablocki have since been breathing new life into the business founded in 1936 by Isadore Mirsky and Morris Kossar.

The bialy is a soft, round bread with a dent in its center. At Kossar's, the dent is filled with bits of onion or garlic. The roll was among the foods brought to the city a century ago by Eastern European Jews. It inspired a book by Mimi Sheraton called *The Bialy Eaters.* "I can't tell you how many times a day a person comes in and *needs* to tell us they've been coming here thirty or forty years," Evan says. "There's something important about preserving these brands and making them prosper. There's no reason Kossar's has to fade away simply because it's old."

LA FRITE, 99 MacDougal St., New York, NY 10011; (917) 388-2541; lafritenyc.com

There are plenty of burger joints that ask if you want fries with your burger, so Adil Fawzi opened a fry joint that asks if you want burgers with your fries. It's a curious twist, but then probably no more curious than the twist of a French chef who wants to run a New York fry joint. Adil left a prestigious career in France to come to New York, where he opened the French spots Bistro 61 and Marché du Sud. Then his wife took him to Amsterdam, where he saw a big line at a little fry shack. He wanted one of those. He opened La Frite in 2013.

And in his first twist, he offered his fries in two different widths. In his second, he offered sauces like his Spinach, Basil & Kale Mayo. In his third, he offered a "signature" topping of bacon crisps. And fourth, he offered a side of sliders: "You have to adjust for the market." Coincidentally, he opened La Frite in the former space of Chipsy, a fry joint that had opened just two years earlier. Besides potatoes, Chipsy fried things like pickles, Oreos, and Twinkies. La Frite is more focused, Adil says: "I really am dedicated to french fries."

LASAGNA RISTORANTE, 941 Second Ave., New York, NY 10022, (212) 308-5353; 196 Eighth Ave., New York, NY 10011, (212) 242-4551; lasagna restaurant.com

Lasagna doesn't have just lasagna, but it may have the most lasagna. Every night it has 17 kinds of lasagna. When you get lasagna, you get a lot of lasagna, which is the right amount. If you're eating something that you think you shouldn't, you might as well eat a lot of it.

Lasagna has eggplant lasagna, spinach lasagna, mushroom lasagna, and asparagus lasagna. It has four-cheese lasagna, hearts-of-artichoke lasagna, and lasagna primavera. It has ground-sirloin lasagna, ground-veal lasagna, sausage-and-onion lasagna, grilled-chicken lasagna, and prosciutto lasagna. That takes care of your meat and vegetables. For your seafood, there are lobster lasagna, grilled-salmon lasagna, and shrimp-and-scallop lasagna. There's always a special lasagna, like goat-cheese-and-sun-dried-tomato lasagna or crabmeat lasagna. And there's always the option of just plain lasagna.

The menu also offers Create Your Own Lasagna, which has led to fearsome creations like veal, spinach, and cream-sauce lasagna. Lasagna's owner, Adam Honig, says he tried to prevent that one: "I told them I thought it was a little over the top. But the customer gets what he wants."

MACBAR, 54 Prince St., New York, NY 10012; (212) 226-8877; macbar.net
The happy duck on the Macbar website quacks to let you know that he's an ingredient in the spot's signature dish, the Mac Quack. It's made with duck confit, Fontina, caramelized onions, herbs, and macaroni, the part of the namesake that doesn't quack.

As Michael Ferraro, the executive chef, points out, Macbar has a double theme. Its menu, he says, "consists of twelve sophisticated twists on classic comfort-food dishes turned into mac and cheese." Its space, accordingly, looks like a big piece of mac and cheese. Besides the Mac Quack, the sophisticated twists include the Mac Stroganoff, with braised beef, stewed mushrooms, and sour-cream sauce; the Mac Lobsta', with lobster, cognac, tarragon, and mascarpone; and the Mac Reuben, with braised corned beef, sauerkraut, Swiss cheese, and rye-bread crumbs.

The spot opened in 2009. It's a spinoff of Delicatessen, next door, where Michael cooks up "international comfort food." Macbar is tiny, but it has a big quack, Michael says, thanks to its yellow packaging: "You can spot someone eating Macbar from a block away."

MANOUSHEH, 193 Bleecker Street, New York, NY 10012; (347) 971-5778; manousheh.com
Ziyad Hermez invites you to make a lunch or a dinner out of a breakfast, and he even invites you to call it a pizza instead of a sandwich. Anything to get you to know and love the preeminent street food of Lebanon. Anything to get you hooked on manousheh.

It's folded into a sandwich, but then it's a flatbread with toppings like pizza. It's a breakfast in Beirut, but then anything goes in New York. In any case, "all the Lebanese here have been waiting for it for so long," Ziyad says, "that when we opened it seemed as if they all walked in here." His savory choices include za'atar, topped with thyme, sumac, and sesame seeds, and jibneh, topped with akkawi cheese. He also has one with za'atar, avocado, cherry tomatoes, mint, olives, and cucumbers. "It's not traditional," he says. "We just like avocados."

Ziyad was going to hire someone to do the manousheh baking until he realized that he really wanted to do it himself. He opened the shop in 2015. And he truly does aim to please: "One of the beauties of a bakery like this is that the baker will hardly ever say no."

THE MEADOW, 523 Hudson St., New York, NY 10014; (212) 645-4633; atthemeadow.com

Say "Pass the salt" to a disciple of The Meadow, and prepare to be asked whether you mean the Himalayan Pink Salt or the Iburi Jio Cherry Smoked Salt. If you mean the Himalayan Pink Salt, prepare to be asked whether you mean the fine, the medium-fine, or the coarse. If you don't know what you mean, prepare to be forgiven. For the typical person, salt is salt, but as Kaitlin Hansen of The Meadow points out, that's like thinking that chocolate is chocolate. There are many salts. The Meadow, for instance, has 130 of them.

Behold the Salt Wall, and behold jars of Carolina Flake Sea Salt, Korean Oyster Bamboo Salt, and Peruvian Warm Spring Finishing Salt. Choose that, and learn that "the pearl-pink crystals of Peru Mountain Spring radiate the beauty of a child's quick laugh rippling from a hut on the banks of the Urubamba River." The point is that better salt makes food taste better. That's why Mark Bitterman began stalking salt. He opened the first Meadow in Oregon, and the second here. Both sell his books, *Salt Block Cooking* and *Salted: A Manifesto on the World's Most Essential Mineral.*

MELT SHOP, 55 W. 26th St., New York, NY 10010, (212) 447-6358; 135 W. 50th St., New York, NY 10019, (212) 974-3423; 601 Lexington Ave., New York, NY 10022, (212) 759-6358; meltshop.com

Melt Shop handles the grilled-cheese turf between "super fancy" and your frying pan, and it's working: Melt keeps opening more shops. It bills itself as a place for "comfort food," or "the food you'd rather have than any other food." But grilled cheese is still its signature food.

It comes as the Classic, which is American on white, to which you can add tomato and caramelized onions, bacon, fried or grilled chicken, or a burger. It comes as the Wisco, which is sharp cheddar, brick spread, bacon, and tomato, and as the Shroom, which is portobello, goat cheese, Havarti, and parsley pesto. It comes in a few other ways, including the Truffle Melt, which is Havarti, truffle oil, and arugula on sourdough. However, it never comes in quite as intricate ways as the grilled cheeses at, say, Little Muenster, which is the place that bills its sandwiches as super fancy.

Spencer Rubin just wanted to get creative with grilled cheese while everyone else was getting creative with burgers. That's why he and Josh Morgan opened Melt Shop, in 2011. He still gets creative, he says, but only to a point: "We want people to look at the menu and know everything on it."

Also try: Amused, 142 W. 83rd St., New York, NY 10024; (212) 799-0080; amusednyc.com (open weekends)

MELTKRAFT, 101 MacDougal St., New York, NY 10012, (212) 380-1275; 442 Ninth St., Brooklyn, NY 11215, (347) 889-6290; meltkraft.com

You could go to the farm for a lambing tour, a shearing tour, or a cheese-making class, or you could go to Meltkraft for a grilled cheddar-cheese, brisket, and macaroni-and-cheese sandwich. It pretty much depends on how far along you want to be on the food chain. This is the operation that gives you the options. "We're milking seven hundred animals; we make thirty cheeses," says Eran Wajswol. "We go straight from the grass to the consumer's mouth." For the grass, you go to New Jersey. For the grilled cheese, you come here.

Powered, as it is, by Eran's Valley Shepherd Creamery, Meltkraft offers what you could call extreme grilled-cheese sandwiches. They include the signature Valley Thunder, which is the one described above, and the Shepherd Classic, made with three cheeses fresh from the cave. Eran opened the Village store in 2014, following the success of his Brooklyn store, which opened in 2013. He invites you to visit the creamery in Long Valley, New Jersey, but he understands if you have to start with the cheddar, brisket, and mac-and-cheese.

Ô MERVEILLEUX, 1509 Second Ave., New York, NY 10075; (646) 681-8688; omerveilleux.com
New York loves a new dessert even if it's an old one, which is why Anne-Sophie Diotallevi brought it the merveilleux. It's a pastry made of two meringue shells covered in whipped cream and then coated with different flavors. It comes from Belgium, the country that brought us fries and waffles. The classic version is coated with shaved dark chocolate. Sophie has added one with white chocolate and one with crushed Speculoos. She also has minis, in flavors like pistachio–green tea: "It's a good way to make people love this cake. They should try it in Belgium, too."

Belgium is where she grew up, and where, as a girl, she had merveilleux from the local pastry shop on Sunday afternoons. Later she made the cakes at her father's restaurant in Brussels. Their name means "marvelous," and they were marvelous enough to get her to bring them here. She has spent years trying to pin down their origin. For now, she has turned to the challenge of selling them to New Yorkers. "When they see the cake, they think it's huge and very heavy," she says. "When they eat it, they say it's like a cloud."

Also try: Aux Merveilleux de Fred, 37 Eighth Ave., New York, NY 10014; (917) 475-1992; auxmerveilleux.com

OLIVIERS & CO., Grand Central Terminal, New York, NY 10017, (212) 973-1472; 249 Bleecker St., New York, NY 10014, (212) 463-7710; 10 Columbus Circle, New York, NY 10019, (212) 757-9877; oliviersandco.com
O & Co., as it's also known, wants you to think of olive oil as wine, though not so you'd order it by the glass. Along with its extra-virgin olive oils, it has an olive-oil sommelier and guided olive-oil tastings. It tells you whether an oil's nose is of artichoke, pine nuts, or cut grass. The chain of 80 stores was launched in France in 1996 and opened its first shop in New York in 2000. It offers olive oils like Tempio Dell'Oro, Galiga e Vetrice, and Castello di Poppiano, which, besides artichoke, has a nose of crushed olive-tree leaves with herbaceous notes.

The shop also has foods like olive-oil ketchup, olive-oil biscuits, olive-oil organic ratatouille, and olive-oil caramelized-onion-and-maple confit, along with soap made with olive oil, decanters made for olive oil, and spatulas, spoons, and salad servers made of olive wood. Typically, the shop has 25 to 30 different olive oils, which come from as many olive-oil producers. Nevertheless, its best-selling product is its premium balsamic vinegar. Close behind is its basil specialty olive oil, a comparative oil bargain.

100 MONTADITOS, 176 Bleecker St., New York, NY 10012; (646) 719-1713; us.100montaditos.com
You might think that it would take years to try a hundred montaditos, assuming that you know what a montadito is. Then again, if you know what it is, you know that it would take only about 16 sittings, at the rate of six per sitting, which is what you know you'll want. A montadito is the tiny sandwich served by this restaurant, which is one of about 300 100 Montaditoses. The chain began in Spain in 2000, came to Miami in 2011, and debuted in New York, in the West Village, in 2013.

The montaditos are numbered and grouped, presumably to leave you time to eat. Number 1 is Serrano ham. Number 2 is chorizo. Number 90 is meatballs, bacon, Parmesan cheese, and marinara sauce. In between are variations on everything from shrimp to pulled pork. There are even dessert montaditos, including Number 99, which is heavy cream and Oreos on chocolate bread. If you don't like choosing, there are samplers for which six montaditos have been chosen. None of them has any Oreos, though. Everything is a trade-off.

PIE FACE, 464 Ninth Ave., New York, NY 10018; (646) 808-1583; pieface.com

The pies at Pie Face not only have faces, but they also talk to you, if you speak their language. They tell you what's behind the face you're planning to eat. It's odd, but not odd enough to have kept the chain from having several stores in Manhattan, at least for a while. It did this by putting a new face on Australian meat pies, which are to Australians roughly what hot dogs are to Americans. With about six dozen stores in Australia, it opened its first in New York in 2012. It got up to eight, but in late 2014 it closed all but this one.

The pies do indeed have faces and they do indeed talk, in the sense that their lip shapes tell you their fillings in code. An S lip means Chunky Steak Pie, an M lip means Mince Beef & Tomato Pie, C is Chicken & Mushroom, T is Tandoori Vegetable, and O is Thai Chicken Curry, though no one's sure why. Along with the savory pies, there are sweet pies, some of which repeat letters. Since coming to New York, the chain has added pies requested by New Yorkers. These include, strangely enough, the Philly Cheesesteak Pie and the BBQ Pulled Pork Pie, or, in pie talk, your Ps and Qs.

POP KARMA, 95 Orchard St., New York, NY 10002; (917) 675-7450; popkarma.com

When it's hot out, you can have Spanish Barbecue ("Summer in a bag"). When it's cold out, you can have Gingerbread Stout Caramel ("Sugar plum fairies on your tongue"). Pop Karma wants you to experience New York's glorious changes of season, even if it's out of a popcorn sack. Pop Karma is the popcorn shop you believe you can trust, since the owner, Jean Tsai, is committed to both popcorn and karma. She believes in good ingredients and good behavior. In the words of her website, she wants "to maximize the taste and health benefits of your popcorn."

It seems to be working. Pop Karma is in its third year in a city that has seen popcorn shops pop in and pop out. They've ranged from Populence, which appeared at the same time as Pop Karma, to Jack's Corn Crib, which goes back to the '80s and whose Jack was the actor Jack Klugman. Among Jean's other seasonal flavors are Margarita and Bacon Apple Bourbon Caramel. But there are always the Classics: Mediterranean, Zen Cheddar, and Pure Caramel. And those are the top pops, Jean says: "I think people just like to hear what the new flavors are."

Also try: Garrett Popcorn Shops, 242 W. 34th St., New York, NY 10119; (888) 476-7267; garrettpopcorn.com

RISOTTERIA, 270 Bleecker St., New York, NY 10014; (212) 924-6664; risotteria.com

Risotto is a creamy rice dish. Risotteria can acquaint you with it. Its menu lists three dozen different versions. They're sorted as Arborio, which has chicken stock; Carnaroli, also with chicken stock; and Vialone Nano, with vegetable stock. You're getting acquainted already. The versions include Arborio with porcini, sweet corn, and white truffle oil; Canaroli with roasted leg of lamb, gorgonzola dolce latte, and spinach; and Vialone Nano with mozzarella and pesto. There are also daily specials, which brings the total closer to four dozen.

The menu once explained not only what risotto is, but also where it's from, where it's found, how it's made, and how you should eat it. It taught you about rice-grain sizes and about rice varieties. It told you why Risotteria uses Arborio, Carnaroli, and Vialone Nano. Now it leaves your risotto education up to you, maybe because the place is small and people were spending too much time reading. It still puts a G next to everything that's gluten-free, which is almost everything, and it leaves your gluten education up to you, too.

SAKAYA, 324 E. Ninth St., New York, NY 10003; (212) 505-7253; sakayanyc.com

Most people who enter Sakaya say "I don't know much about sake." Rick Smith welcomes them, for he was one of them—even when he worked for a wine magazine. "I thought all sake was hot, high in alcohol, and nasty," he says. Eventually he learned the truth, and now he spreads it. Sake is a beverage that is made from fermented rice and that, in Rick's words, "is brewed like beer and drinks like wine." Sakaya sells premium sake, and that's a premium for New York. There are just four sake stores in the country, Rick says, and the other three are out West.

At Sakaya, which Rick runs with his wife, Hiroko Furukawa, you learn that sake is graded on a rice-polishing scale, but that a low grade doesn't mean a bad sake. You learn that not all good sake has to be served cold, but that all bad sake should probably be served hot. Of the popular Dassai 50 "Otter Fest," you learn that the rice-polishing rate is 50 percent, that it pairs well with oysters, and that it's best chilled. Those are the sorts of things you can learn about each of the store's 150 sakes. But the main thing, probably, is that none of them is nasty.

SINGAPORE MALAYSIA BEEF JERKY, 95A Elizabeth St., New York, NY 10013; (212) 965-0796; malaysiabeefjerky.com

Many people are surprised to find that there's a store devoted to jerky. They'd be even more surprised to find that there are a few stores devoted to jerky. Each of the stores, moreover, has its own jerky style, but Singapore Malaysia is a fine choice for the jerky novice. It's a storefront that's easy to miss; you have to look up to see the awning with the red silhouettes of the chicken, the pig, and the cow. After you do, look back down, peer into the window, and see an arm turning dozens of pieces of jerky on a grill. These ain't Slim Jims.

Walk in, breathe the aroma, and feast your eyes on display cases piled with glowing sliced-meat jerky and ground-meat jerky. In both styles, there's beef, pork, spicy beef, and spicy pork. In sliced, there's also shrimp with pork. In ground, there's also chicken and spicy chicken.

The place began with just beef, says Ricky Wong, a store worker. Customers asked for other flavors, and the store obliged. The window grill, he says, lets "people see what we're doing." He, too, lets people see what he's doing: snipping the charred edges off the meat "for health."

TAQUITORIA, 168 Ludlow St., New York, NY 10002; (212) 780-0121; taquitoria.com

Matthew Conway said: "You can get everything you dream of in New York except good taquitos." Barry Frish said: "I don't even know what a good taquito looks like." It was as good a start as any, so they called their friend Brad Holtzman, and the three guys decided to open a taquito restaurant. A taquito is a cigar-sized, deep-fried taco, and Taquitoria makes it easy to get hold of a few of them fast. You pick beef, chicken, pork, or black beans. You pick a Classic, which has guac sauce, shredded lettuce, and cotija cheese, or a Cheesy, with sour cream, nacho cheese, and pickled jalapeño relish.

That's it. You order three or five, and in moments, you're experiencing what Brad describes as their "crunchy cheesy deliciousness." "A lot of people have never had a taquito and don't know what they are, so we're opening their eyes to something new," he says. "The crunch always gets them." It's what got Matthew, who had discovered taquitos in San Diego and kept them in mind while he, Barry, and Brad worked at Restaurant Marc Forgione. Within minutes of their decision, Brad says, "we had a flight booked to San Diego to do what we call research and development, which means eating and drinking a *ton*."

THE ONE-*THING* WONDERS

Sell shoes, and you were out. Sell huaraches, and you were in. That was roughly the major guideline for admittance to this section. Unfortunately, if there's a shop in New York that sells only huaraches, I missed it, but if I had found it, it would be here. This is the place for stores that sell only things that are not normally found in stores of their own, if they are normally found in stores at all.

A place that sells nothing but sushi is not necessarily a one-food wonder, while a place that sells nothing but vegetarian sushi is. Likewise, a place that sells nothing but clothes is not necessarily a one-thing wonder, while a place that sells nothing but hoodies is.

In other words, this is not the place to find an outdoor-goods store, a musical-instrument store, a leather store, or a bicycle store. It is the place to find an umbrella store, an accordion store, a design-your-own-belt store, and a mostly-1980s vintage-bicycle store. You'll find a regular record store, because it's close to the only one left. You won't find a regular bookstore, at least not yet. You will find a couple of all-food bookstores, and if there's a second edition of this book, you may by then find a regular bookstore.

I chose stores that I saw as the most suited to general use, which is why I didn't choose, say, the all-feather store or the all-zipper store. I did choose the all-button store, because you have a better chance of seeing, say, Humphrey Bogart on a button than on a feather or a zipper. In short, picking one-thing wonders is trickier than picking one-food wonders, especially when you're the one who's defining the term. But even if you believe that I was wrong to exclude the feather store, you can't deny that I was right to include the chopsticks store.

ALEX & BELL ACCORDIONS, 165 W. 48th St., New York, NY 10036; (212) 819-0072; alexmusical.com

The twin mermaids with the strategically placed red rhinestones await you in the Alex Accordion Museum, which is part of the Alex & Bell Accordions store. So even if you're not currently in need of an accordion, you can find compelling diversion in this accordion emporium. The mermaids grace what is labeled the "E. Galizi Bro. White-and-Gold Pearled Piano Accordion," which Alex says was made in New York in the '20s. Alex is Alessandro Carozza, the curator of the museum, the proprietor of the store, and the Accordion King.

   In his two-floor complex, he buys, sells, repairs, and otherwise tends to accordions that span about a century. Still, he loves to show off his museum—and he's grateful for his museum, because moving his accordions there from his apartment kept his wife from leaving him. He's been selling accordions for decades, but he still buys them by the hundreds. He can't retire: "They don't let me—the professionals," he says. "They need me, and I have to do it. They come from so far. . . . They say, 'Don't die, Alex, 'cause if you die, we don't play anymore.'"

BADICHI CUSTOMIZED BELTS, 159 Prince St., New York, NY 10012; 637 Broadway, New York, NY 10012; 367 W. Broadway, New York, NY 10013; 298 Bleecker St., New York, NY 10014; 205 W. 57th St., New York, NY 10019; (212) 533-2107; badichibelts.com

A city with so much opportunity to build your own meals needs a place where you can build your own belt to go around them. Fortunately, Yinon Badichi left Jerusalem and moved to New York just to supply that place, even if it had nothing to do with the meals. At Badichi, you choose a strap, you choose a buckle, you choose a size, and someone turns your choices into a belt. The straps come in most imaginable colors, styles, patterns, and textures. The buckles come in most imaginable things, from knight shields to kissing seahorses.

"Today, in order to succeed in business you need to be avant-garde, you need to be creative, you need to be different," Yinon says of his concept. "There's a do-it-yourself trend; everyone wants to define himself. And the big fashion companies weren't giving belts the right attention." He's making up for it. A few years later, he's up to five stores, and he's envisioning Badichis everywhere. The belts' price range is wide—from $40 to $1,000—and their uses are varied. Yinon says that one client bought 15 belts for what the client referred to as "my mistresses around the world."

BOND NO. 9, 9 Bond St., New York, NY 10012; 863 Washington St., New York, NY 10014; 399 Bleecker St., New York, NY 10014; 897 Madison Ave., New York, NY 10021; (877) 273-3369; bondno9.com

For those special times when you simply have to smell like Bryant Park, you simply have to go to Bond No. 9—for a bottle of Bryant Park. You might as well go there, too, when you simply have to smell like Chinatown, Astor Place, Washington Square, Park Avenue, or Central Park West. All those locales and more have bottles of their own, because Bond No. 9 is the company that takes the scents out of New York. It captures an area's essence and turns it into a perfume, allowing you to exude the myriad fragrances of the city that always smells.

Little Italy is "citrus-flavored melt-in-your-mouth gelato in spray form." Wall Street is "a cool, zesty, spicy androgynous career scent." Central Park South has "top notes of grapefruit flower and blackcurrant buds," though wisely no notes of carriage-ride horse.

The collection was created by Laurice Rahmé, a French perfume expert who was inspired by this aromatic town. It comprises 61 scents for men, women, or both, and it keeps growing, so you never know what's next. Imagine the top notes of Meatpacking District.

BONNIE SLOTNICK COOKBOOKS, 28 E. Second St., New York, NY 10003; (212) 989-8962; bonnieslotnickcookbooks.com

Whether you favor lamb loaf, ham loaf, or yam loaf, you'll find it in *Meat-loaf*, even though yam is not a meat. The book, by Sharon Moore, is among the curious volumes that bubble up at Bonnie Slotnick Cookbooks, the little shop where old cookbooks go to feel young. Like the city's other food-book stores, Bonnie's place has aged into something all its own. It's a homey place packed mostly with out-of-print 20th-century cookbooks that can put food on the table in ways that not even New York restaurants can.

It has *The Apple Cookbook, The Walnut Cookbook, The Cruising Cookbook*, and *The Commune Cookbook*. It also has *The James Beard Cook Book, The Dinah Shore Cook Book*, and multiple versions of its most popular volumes, the Betty Crocker cookbooks. Festooning the space are useful vintage kitchen aids, like the Acme Rotary Mincer and Betty Brite Bake Cups. But if it's Coca-Cola Chicken you want, you'll need Carolyn Wyman's *The Kitchen Sink Cookbook*—which can also supply you with Chocolate Cricket Torte.

CASEY RUBBER STAMPS, 322 E. 11th St., New York, NY 10003; (917) 669-4151; caseyrubberstamps.com

Why you want a rubber stamp of Humpty Dumpty is your business. Seeing to it that you're supplied with that stamp is John Casey's. He'll make you a rubber stamp of anything, though chances are good that whatever rubber stamp you want, he's already made it. The two long walls of his narrow shop are veritable mosaics of the hundreds and hundreds of rubber stamps he has in stock. They include peacocks and mountain goats, peapods and corncobs, boneshakers and station wagons, eyes, ears, and feet—and Humpty Dumptys.

As a kid, John was taken with coins until he saw a coin on a printer's block. He's been making his stamps in New York since 1979. He has molds for thousands of stamps that aren't on display. He also sells ink pads, in colors including box brown, sunflower, and eggplant.

He has learned that nothing's too strange for a stamp: "We had a girl who was going to art classes, and she had mousetraps with dried-out mice in them. She made a drawing of the dried-out, mummified mice and had a rubber stamp made of it. Then she made wallpaper with it."

Also try: The Ink Pad, 37 Seventh Ave., New York, NY 10011; (212) 463-9876; theinkpadnyc.com

CHARTWELL BOOKSELLERS, 55 E. 52nd St., New York, NY 10055; (212) 308-0643; churchillbooks.com

There was once a bookstore in the city that specialized in biographies. Chartwell saw that niche as too broad—so it specialized in Winston Churchill biographies. Though it still has titles on other topics, its subtitle tells its story: "The World's Only Winston Churchill Bookshop." Barry Singer presides over the myriad shelves devoted to the leader who has inspired several hundred biographies, and who wrote 42 books himself. Churchill deserves a store, he says, not only because he saved the world, but also because he was fascinating. He saved the world *and* raised butterflies.

Chartwell opened as a general bookstore in 1983. The building's owner, Robert Fisher, named it for Churchill's home. With that name, Barry figured, it ought to have Churchill books. He got them. Eventually he wrote one: *Churchill Style: The Art of Being Winston Churchill.*

That old biography bookshop, which was called Biography Bookshop, has become a general bookshop, whose name is bookbook. Nevertheless, Barry says, along with the world Churchill saved Chartwell: "If we didn't specialize very narrowly in Churchill, we'd be gone."

THE DRAMA BOOK SHOP, 250 W. 40th St., New York, NY 10018; (212) 944-0595; dramabookshop.com

By theatrical standards, The Drama Book Shop has been a smash. It's been running for 98 years—and it's won a Tony. The 2011 award was "for service to our community as a storied emporium of play scripts, periodicals, and all manner of theater books since 1917." If you'd like to win a Tony, you'll probably end up shopping here. It's the place where aspiring actors find the vehicles to act in. Though it does have all manner of theater books, about half of its 20,000 titles are plays. The main thing that a play has to do to get in here is to be written.

"The store was started by The Drama League on a card table in a theater," says Allen Hubby, the current owner. It left the League six years later. It was eventually run by Arthur and Rozanne Seelen, Allen's uncle and aunt. Arthur died in 2000, but Rozanne still makes appearances. The store has been in its current location since 2001, and it's dealing with current bookstore challenges—minus one, Allen says. "We hear from customers that directors say, 'Do not get the play on a Kindle.' They can't deal with stopping a rehearsal because someone's battery's dead."

FOUNTAIN PEN HOSPITAL, 10 Warren St., New York, NY 10007; (212) 964-0580; fountainpenhospital.com

There aren't that many patients these days, which is understandable, since there also aren't that many fountain pens these days. These days, the Fountain Pen Hospital is less a medical facility than it is the last major pen store left in New York. It has ballpoints, of course, since it wasn't much more likely to survive on just fountain pens than on just fountain-pen surgery. It has thousands of pens. Those still include lots of fountain pens, along with fountain-pen cases, fountain-pen ink, and fountain-pen nibs.

The place was launched, as mostly a hospital, in 1946 by Albert Wiederlight and his son Phillip. It's now in the hands of Phillip's sons Steve and Terry Wiederlight, who supply pen aficionados with their Auroras,

Montblancs, Sheaffers, and Watermans. The aficionados are on the mature side, Terry acknowledges: "We're not getting much of the younger generation." You can help, he adds: "It's a great gift. Give somebody a bottle of liquor, they drink it, and it's over. Give them a nice pen, and they use it and they think about you."

GEORGE GLAZER GALLERY, 308 E. 94th St., New York, NY 10128; (212) 535-5706; georgeglazer.com

You can't argue with the universality of the globe. It's something that most of the people you know live on. That's part of what George Glazer was thinking when he opened up a globe store. It was a good thought: George Glazer Gallery has been around for over a decade. George has hundreds of globes, mostly from the 18th through 20th centuries, mostly from $200 to $100,000. He has pocket globes, novelty globes, table globes, and floor globes. He has orreries, tellurians, and Ptolemaic armillary spheres.

He loves globes, he says, and he figures that everyone else at least likes them: "It's hard not to like one. You don't hear anyone saying, 'Oh, I really don't like that globe.'" Still, among a few other things, his gallery sells maps, presumably for people who prefer the world flat.

George has globes for many needs, including a thermometer globe, and globes for many spaces—they go up to 30 inches. Just measure your entrance for that big one, he warns: "It's not like a couch that you can jimmy around the corner. It's thirty inches, no matter which way you turn it."

THE HOODIE SHOP, 181 Orchard St., New York, NY 10002; (646) 559-2716; thehoodieshop.com

Since it's The Hoodie Shop, you could say that its specialty is the hoodie, but on closer inspection you could say that its specialty is the hood. Along with sweatshirts with a hood, which is what you may think of as a hoodie, it has other things with a hood that you may never have thought of. It has T-shirts with a hood and bathing suits with a hood. It has scarves with a hood and leather jackets with a hood. It has dresses with a hood and blazers with a hood and suit jackets with a hood. Whatever you choose here, the shop ensures that it'll go over your head.

"I found it fascinating that there's this article of clothing that everyone has in their closet . . . and there wasn't a store devoted to that," says Aleah Speranza. So she created a store for that article, which she says is a store for everyone, since "everyone has a perception of what a hoodie should stand for." Her partners are Peter Shapiro, the owner of the legendary Brooklyn Bowl, and Questlove of The Roots, the band of *The Tonight Show Starring Jimmy Fallon*. Accordingly, the shop has live music and a '60s-rock motif. "It's not just a store," Aleah explains. "It's its own little medium."

HOUSE OF OLDIES, 35 Carmine St., New York, NY 10014; (212) 243-0500; houseofoldies.com

Finding a record store was once a snap. Now it's a miracle. Especially if the record store you find sells only records. Thirty years ago, House of Oldies posted a sign that said "No CD's / No Tapes / Just Records." The sign is still up. The policy is still in effect.

The shop awning says "Rare Records," which is now arguably redundant. Either way, the shop stocks nothing but 33s and 45s. Most are rock 'n' roll, pop, soul, rhythm and blues, doo-wop, and blues, and most span the mid-20th century. But there tends to be a little of everything.

The House opened in '62. Since then the city, like the country, has seen the birth and death of countless record stores, record chains, and record departments. House of Oldies has outlived them all. So has Bob Abramson, who's been in there pushing the platters almost from the start. He still sells the records that he sold 40 years ago, not just to adults dissatisfied with CDs, but also to teens dissatisfied with downloads. "They love the sound of vinyl," Bob says with an air of triumph. "They'll come in and say, 'Got any Zeppelin on wax?'"

IDLEWILD BOOKS, 12 W. 19th St., New York, NY 10011; (212) 414-8888; idlewildbooks.com

Idlewild's the place from which you embark upon your trip around the world, whether you're going anywhere or not. That's why it took on the former name of the airport now known as JFK. It's a travel-book store that lets you get to know countries through more than travel books. If your destination is France, for instance, you travel to the store's France section, where—along with guidebooks and language books related to France—you can find novels, mysteries, biographies, poetry books, cookbooks, and children's books related to France.

David Del Vecchio opened the store in 2008, offering a counterpoint to The Complete Traveller Antiquarian Bookstore, which sold old travel books. David had been a press officer at the United Nations, which may or may not have played a part in his literary wanderlust. In 2010 he started offering foreign-language books and classes. They do their part to support the store. They don't do much, though, to help customers who are short on airport history. "Most people under forty," David says, "have no idea where our name came from."

JEAN'S SILVERSMITHS, 16 W. 45th St., New York, NY 10036; (212) 575-0723; jeanssilversmiths.com

When you're one fork short of a place setting, this is the place to replace it, especially if your scanty place setting is sterling. Jean's is a storehouse for silver in most of its glimmering forms, from lapel pins to loving cups. Chances are good that it stores what you're missing. Its specialty is silver-matching; it boasts more than a thousand patterns, and if it doesn't have yours, it knows where to look. Along with flatware, it has hollowware, such as gravy boats, punch bowls, and tea sets, along with assorted pill boxes, nail buffers, and asparagus trays.

It looks like a curiosity shop, which is what it once was: the Park Curiosity Shop, which opened in 1910. According to legend, in the '30s Armand Guior renamed it for the silver-swiping Jean Valjean after seeing *Les Misérables* (the Fredric March version). The store moved in 1958, and in 1999 it was taken over by three employees, including Armand's nephew David Shaw. David now reveals that he is the answer to the question most frequently asked by people who are dazed by the shop's profusion of silver: "Who polishes this?"

JJ HAT CENTER, 310 Fifth Avenue, New York, NY 10001; (212) 239-4368; jjhatcenter.com
JJ will steam your hat for free, which sounds like a fabulous offer, until you take a moment to realize that you don't own a hat worth steaming. In which case JJ can supply you with a steam-worthy hat wardrobe, which will include no hats with plastic adjustment straps.

That's because JJ is the last of the traditional men's hat shops in Manhattan, which, just a few decades ago, had dozens. It fits men with everything from top hats and trilbies to boaters and buckets, and it does so in fittingly manly surroundings: a showroom with oak and a fireplace.

The store is descended from one that opened in 1911 on Herald Square, which went through a few names and owners. It was a struggling survivor in the '70s, when it was rescued by father-and-son hat men. Both were John Joseph Lambert, but instead of JJJJ, they went with JJ. The son, Jack Lambert, moved the store in 1995, and soon after, passed it along to his manager, Aida O'Toole. Aida has opened two smaller stores, in the East Village and Williamsburg, called Pork Pie Hatters, named for the chapeau of the New York sewer-worker Ed Norton.

JOANNE HENDRICKS, COOKBOOKS, 488 Greenwich St., New York, NY 10013; (212) 226-5731; joannehendrickscookbooks.com
When you enter her store, Joanne Hendricks might be polishing the pewter, not only because it's her pewter, but because it's her house. Her cookbook

shop is on the first floor of the two-century-old brick house where she's lived and run the shop since 1975. She bills her books as "antiquarian, out-of-print, and unusual." They span roughly the same two centuries as the house. They include titles like *A Treatise on the Art of Boiling Sugar*. They are treasures not unlike the pewter, she says: "My whole family likes to have pretty things."

Among her treasures are Geraldene Holt's *Cake Stall* (1980), *Famous New Orleans Drinks and How to Mix 'Em* (1947), and *Manuel Du Vinaigrier Et Du Moutardier* (1827), a French book whose English title would be *Manual of Vinegar and Mustard*.

Joanne moved to New York from New Jersey and worked at Ruby's Book Sale, a Tribeca fixture that closed in 2005. At Ruby's she favored the cookbooks, and she's always favored the unusual, but she sells the usual, too, she says: "I have a nice macaroni section."

JUST BULBS, 220 E. 60th St., New York, NY 10022; (212) 888-5707; justbulbsnyc.com

A woman in Tennessee favored soft-pink lightbulbs, because she believed that they gave her complexion a rosy glow. "She bought twelve hundred pieces, because she didn't want to ever run out of them," says David Brooks, the owner of the place that she called for them: Just Bulbs. David is the son of Shirley Brooks, who launched the store in 1980. Shirley is the daughter of Abraham Brachfeld, who launched the business in 1942. Abraham shlepped through the Empire State Building, peddling and changing bulbs. Shirley decided to let the bulb-buyers do the shlepping.

The store has bulbs with such illuminating names as Eggplant, Grapefruit, Ping-Pong, Vertical Pigtail, Cocktail Frank, and Pinprick Balls. It also has immortality through a video clip in which David Letterman tries to understand exactly what it is that the store sells:

"The name of the store is Just Bulbs, and that's exactly what we sell—just bulbs."

"So besides bulbs, what do you have here?"

"Nothing."

"How about shades? Could you get shades here?"

"No, we are just bulbs. If you want shades, maybe you go to a place called Just Shades."

JUST SHADES, 21 Spring St., New York, NY 10012; (212) 966-2757; justshadesny.com

If you sell just shades, you can stock more shades than you could if you also had to sell lamps. This apparently was the premise on which Anne Rakower opened her lampshade store, and the store's been softening the hard glare of life for about half a century now. It's still faithful to the premise, stocking around 5,000 shades. It has your drum shades and your string shades, your bell shades and your bouillotte shades. It makes tourists jealous, says the current owner, Marc Engelson: "They say, 'You should open in Wichita,' 'You should open in Chicago,' 'You should open in France.'"

Marc says he's come up with everything from a 3-inch shade for a table lamp to an 8-foot shade for a restaurant fixture. (That one couldn't get through the door.) He has finials, but otherwise it's just shades, as David Letterman learned when he popped in, following his visit to Just Bulbs:

"What is the name of this store?"

"Just Shades."

"And what can you get in here?"

"'What can you *get* in here?' The shades. That's why our name is Just Shades."

"But seriously—what can you get besides shades here?"

KAAS GLASSWORKS, 117 Perry Street, New York, NY 10014; (212) 366-0322; kaas.com

From finches to fig berries, from woodwinds to wine bottles, from Napoleon to Santa Claus—and anyone in between—Carol Kaas puts everything under the sun under glass at Kaas Glassworks, a tiny shop devoted to the rarefied art of glass-tray decoupage. Working from vintage prints and other paper that she extracts from estate sales and flea markets, her artists glue images to the bottoms of clear trays of assorted sizes and shapes. The results have ended up everywhere from modest coffee tables to the comparatively immodest Academy Awards.

The shop is chockablock with finished trays, but at least half its business comes from custom orders, for which patrons bring in paper of their own. Carol has sent out trays displaying marriage certificates, birth announcements, kids' drawings, and "a proposal on the back of a Starbucks coffee cup."

She didn't aim for this. She studied art, but she became a lawyer. She practiced for 15 years, including 10 as a prosecutor. But she found herself doing decoupage "out of our kitchen sink." She can't resist it, she says: "I love taking those images and bringing them back to life."

KITCHEN ARTS & LETTERS, 1435 Lexington Ave., New York, NY 10128; (212) 876-5550; kitchenartsandletters.com

If you think of this as a cookbook store, you're robbing yourself of the chance to discover a book that tells you how to launch your own mango orchard. "The idea was to have a single subject and provide breadth," says the owner, Nach Waxman. "It's a store that's about the world of food and wine." That makes it a store for everyone, but particularly a store for everyone who inhabits that world, which it has been since Julia Child ambled in at the start. More than half the customers are the likes of chefs, restaurateurs, food writers, food editors, food teachers, food historians, and food scholars.

"If you want a book on ancient Roman food poetry, we have that book," Nach says. "If you want a book on the role of gastronomy in the plays of Molière, we have that book. We have books on hydrocolloids and enzymes. We have a dictionary of Chinese food plants."

It once might have been a dictionary of Chinese badminton; sports was high on Nach's list of potential bookstore specialties. But he seems to have made the right choice, since he made it in 1983. "Nobody," he says, "shleps up to Ninety-fourth Street and Lexington Avenue unless they have some real motivation to do so."

LANDMARK VINTAGE BICYCLES, 43 Avenue A, New York, NY 10009; (212) 674-2343; landmarkbicycles.com

Chung Pai made a film called *Love on a Bicycle*. While he was making the film, he fell in love with bicycles. Specifically, he fell in love with old bicycles, which he found more charming than new bicycles. This is how Chung Pai came to open Landmark Vintage Bicycles. He buys and restores old bikes, especially Schwinns and Raleighs, and sells them to cyclists who share his bicycle taste. He has old Schwinn Breezes (for girls), old Schwinn Speedsters (for boys), old Raleigh Sports and Roadsters, and bells for the handlebars.

"Old" at Landmark mostly means 30 to 40 years old, which means that "vintage" includes Japanese brands like Nishiki and Panasonic. The shop has had classics from the '50s and '60s, and from as far back as the '30s, but these days, Chung says, the new vintage is the '80s. "It's hard to beat an old eighties midlevel road bike," he says. And its appeal, apparently, transcends its charm: "They're just as light as new bicycles, and they're cheaper. And people feel more comfortable leaving them outside locked up. They don't get stolen as fast."

THE MYSTERIOUS BOOKSHOP, 58 Warren St., New York, NY 10007; (212) 587-1011; mysteriousbookshop.com

Here's a mystery: Why did New York's other mystery bookstores disappear? At least four have closed in the span of about a decade. Here's another: Why is The Mysterious Bookshop the only one left? Well, it seems possible that the solution to both is Otto Penzler.

Otto is no mystery; besides a mystery seller, he's a mystery editor, a mystery publisher, and a mystery critic. He cowrote the *Encyclopedia of Mystery and Detection*. He edits *The Best American Mystery Stories*. He has worked with Elmore Leonard. He has published Raymond Chandler.

In any case, the city has lost stores with worthy names like Black Orchid, Foul Play, Murder Ink, and Partners & Crime. But Mysterious still dispenses books of mystery, suspense, and crime, as it has since it opened in April 1979, on Friday the 13th. It has a specialty within its specialty: The shop's entire back wall is devoted to Sherlock Holmes and Arthur Conan Doyle. Sherlock is the number-one seller, and number two is a fitting surprise: It's the bibliomysteries, which are, in Otto's words, "mysteries set in the world of books."

RAIN OR SHINE, 45 E. 45th St., New York, NY 10017; (212) 741-9650; rainorshine.biz

Rain or Shine is the umbrella store that understands that you get a hot head, which is why it also has parasols, which is why it's called Rain or Shine. It's an umbrella store that sells umbrellas unlike the kinds whose skeletal remains you see poking out of litter baskets when it rains. It sells umbrellas with names coveted by umbrella connoisseurs, names like Ombrelli Maglia Francesco of Italy and Fox Umbrellas Ltd. of England. Fox has made umbrellas not only for British royalty and for President Kennedy, but also for John Steed of *The Avengers*.

Once you could get such umbrellas at the legendary Uncle Sam, but it closed in 2000 (see this book's Singular Hall of Fame). Peggy Levee went there for a parasol and got inspired by the manager. In 2003 she opened her store—which has the same challenge as Uncle Sam. "Unfortunately, today people just think umbrellas should be cheap and disposable," she says. "Women want something they can just throw in their bag." Instead, they could have a lifelong friend: "They don't understand. If they actually used a good umbrella, it would make such a difference."

SERMONETA GLOVES, 609 Madison Ave., New York, NY 10022; (212) 319-5946; sermonetagloves.com

When you walk into Sermoneta, you feel like they're giving you a hand, even though, in a sense, you're giving them yours. Give freely and you can walk out with your hands in anything from napa full-finger unlined driving gloves to peccary-leather Orylag-fur-lined zippered gloves. In this New York boutique of the Italian glove chainlet, the gloves are posed upright, hand in hand, as if they're applauding your refined taste. More likely, they're standing tall to show off their colors, leathers, linings, trimmings, and styles. These are worldly gloves.

Some people come in to get gloves that stand out; others come in to get gloves that blend in. Among the members of that second group are debutantes, says Kara Lee Kelly, the boutique's general manager: "They get gloves for cotillions. They all get white-leather opera-length gloves." Business can be tough in the summer, though there are cotton sun gloves. But most of the year, Kara says, the store can depend on its regulars. "There are women who come in once a week to buy gloves," she says. "There are women who come in to buy gloves for the outfit they're wearing that day."

TENDER BUTTONS, 143 E. 62nd St., New York, NY 10065; (212) 758-7004; tenderbuttons-nyc.com

It's a button store, but it's where dreams come true—or where dreams at least get closure. "We recently sold buttons in the shapes of fruits and vegetables to the head of a vegetarian society," says Millicent Safro, the button tender. "We provided a card of lion buttons for someone whose husband's name is Leo. We provided fox buttons for Mrs. Fox."

That's what you do when you have a million buttons. You provide baseball buttons, bottle-cap buttons, Brando buttons, and Bogart buttons. You also read about buttons, write about buttons, and root around for buttons. Millicent has been doing all of these since 1964. She joined her friend Diana Epstein in launching the store, whose namesake is the book by Gertrude Stein. They moved it to the current spot in 1968. The shop is like a little old library, except that what packs the shelves are cardboard boxes bearing descriptions like "Darling White Frog From England."

Diana died in 1998, but the place hasn't changed. That's why Peg Hewitt of Illinois dreamed of visiting. Her dream came true when she was 95. She visited. She bought buttons. "She was really, really happy," Millicent says. "She died the following day on the way home."

YUNHONG CHOPSTICKS, 50 Mott St., New York, NY 10013; (212) 566-8828; happychopsticks.com; 235 Canal St., New York, NY 10013; (917) 603-1936

You wouldn't like scraping your knife and fork together to avoid getting splinters in your lips. But you accept doing that with chopsticks, or at least you tolerate it, at least for takeout. Sure, some restaurants give you no choice, but Yunhong Chopsticks more than makes up for them.

Yunhong gives you hundreds of choices of chopsticks—all splinter-free, and all meant to last a lifetime instead of a lunchtime. They are displayed on the walls like artwork, which most of them are. The store says chopsticks are a gift of happiness, and that's especially true for your lips. You can get wooden Chinese Zodiac Chopsticks for just a few bucks, or Mother of Pearl Mahogany Chopsticks for over 200. There are Seashell Inlays Chopsticks, Huali Wood with Silver Chopsticks, Faces of Opera Chopsticks, and Chairman Mao's Famous Phrases Chopsticks.

Yunhong opened in 2008 as part of a Chinese chain. It's billed as "the first chopsticks boutique ever in the United States." And it's a good place to get started with chopsticks: It has Children Training Chopsticks, complete with finger loops and gaily colored animal heads.

THE NEW YORK SINGULAR HALL OF FAME

They call me Mr. Yams, or at least they did. I'm not sure it was a sign of respect, though it was more than I usually get. This occurred years ago at my favorite diner in the city, which had yams on its menu but never in its kitchen. I ordered them every week anyway. Soon, whenever I walked in the door, the staff would yell "Mr. Yams!" I was Norm, except Norm got his beer.

It was amusing but tragic, since I really did want the yams. I prize them because they're the only food I enjoy that's nontoxic. Imagine my glee when a man named Hirokazu Sakai opened a restaurant named Hero's Sweet Potatoes. That's right. His name was Hero.

Hero sold baked Japanese sweet potatoes for $2, and they were always perfect. Each came with a free topping, or in the menu's word, a "sause." You could have your sweet potato with cinnamon sugar, with maple syrup, with peanut butter, with chocolate sauce, or sause. I blissfully planned my future.

Unfortunately, my future was to last but one year. After that, Hero closed my sweet-potato sanctuary. He reportedly had visa issues. I sympathized, but his problems seemed minor compared with the ones I faced in returning to my old life as the yamless Mr. Yams.

The moral of the story, of course, is "Everything must go." Nothing lasts forever, especially in New York. In *Discovering Vintage New York* I warn readers not to delay visits to the places they want to see. The same warning applies here. Gather ye yams while ye may.

To drive home the point, if I haven't already, I hereby present what I am confident is the first and only New York Singular Hall of Fame. It commemorates the city's quirkiest single-specialty spots that have vanished in the past few decades. I think they deserve this. Among them you're sure to find places that you wish were still around. Let that be a lesson to you, whatever that lesson is. Maybe it's "Here's an opportunity to reopen these places yourself." If you agree, please start with my yam shop. Just make sure your visa's in order.

THE ONE-FOOD HALL OF FAME

BLINTZ, was at 81 Third Avenue
In parts of the East Village, blintzes are bountiful. Blintz's owner apparently read that as an opportunity. Here blintzes weren't just on the menu; blintzes were the menu. It was all blintzes all the time—or at least till 3 a.m. on weekends. Not just blintzes, but "More than 25 kinds of blintzes," a curious slogan since Blintz actually had more than 35 kinds of blintzes. They included Eggplant and Farmer Cheese; Mushroom and Sour Cream; and Baby Cabbage and Farmer Cheese Topped With an Onion and Paprika Sauce. They also included hot sweet blintzes like Coconut Cream, and cold sweet blintzes like Chocolate Cream With Chocolate Liqueur. But in the end, it's more likely that anyone hungry for a blintz just went to a nearby diner for a nice plain blintz.

BULGIN' WAFFLES CAFÉ, was at 49½ First Avenue
It's easy enough to get waffles, but far less easy to get "waffles so light you need a Magic Carpet to eat one," even if you're not sure what that means. That's what was proffered at Bulgin' Waffles, a place odd enough to merit the odd address of the lamented odd gift shop Little Rickie. A Bulgin' Waffle was 10 inches by 4 inches. A Wafflette was 3 inches by 3 inches. The Bulgin' was "thick and fluffy," while the Wafflette was "thin and delicate." Still, you could have either in batters including whole wheat, buckwheat, pumpkin, banana, pecan, almond, hazelnut, and the enigmatic "non-dairy." The toppings, besides the expected, included Bulgin' Dulce de Leche and Bulgin' Yummy Fudge Sauce, not to mention Ice Cream Slab. Still, the place may just not have fit in a district where people like their snacks portable. Even though it did have a takeout selection called Hot Waffle in a Bag.

CHIPPERY, was on Eighth Street, 23rd Street, and LaGuardia Place

Somebody sometime was going to open an all-potato-chip restaurant, and around the start of this century somebody did. The Chipperys were the New York outposts of a Canadian firm with the reasonable idea of serving potato chips hot, in bowls—that is to say, straight from the oil. Each store had its own potato-chip machine, ejecting chips at the right rate to keep the supply fresh. The chips came in flavors including Ketchup, Dill, B-B-Q, Cajun, Jalapeño, and Cheez-E-Onion. One customer suggested that they try Liver. The chips were apparently popular, but the operation faced myriad challenges, including that of getting enough of the right potatoes for the machines. The Chipperys finally crumbled, but at least there was a bright side: The stores closed before they had enough time to try Liver.

CHOCOLATE PHOTOS, was at 200 W. 57th Street

Victor Syrmis spent two years devising an intricate process for getting an etching of your face onto a 1-inch square of chocolate. In 1982 he launched Chocolate Photos, through which he sold you a box of 24 chocolates with your face and name on each square. He couldn't fully explain the quest but he did his best for me, and I assumed he knew what he was talking about, since he was a psychiatrist: "After twelve years of psychiatry, I got caught in an oral-aggressive state and found the only way to solve my problems was to eat 'em." For a while, he ate well. A few years later the St. Moritz Chocolatier on Madison Avenue used a machine to airbrush your face onto white chocolate. Now, in the digital age, a 3D printer can do the job, but as with all major quests, where would we be without the pioneers?

GURU SNO-BALLS, was at 371 Lafayette Street

A sno-ball, as opposed to a sno-cone, is a confection consisting of snow, as opposed to ice, served in a cup and drenched with flavored syrup. The snow is made by a sno-ball machine. The machine was invented in New Orleans, the home of the sno-ball, as opposed to the snowball. In 1996 Mary Frey of New Orleans brought the sno-ball to New York. She opened Guru in an ex–gas station that she painted chartreuse. She had 50 flavors, including tangerine, lychee, and banana cream pie. She also had Doggie Balls in Chicken and Beefy. Guru was her Rottweiler. A couple of years later, Mary moved on. In 2011 Neesa Peterson, also of New Orleans, brought the balls back. She ran her Imperial Woodpecker Sno-Balls in various locations for three summers, but now she's back in New Orleans—leaving New York with only actual snow.

HERO'S SWEET POTATOES, was at 30 E. 13th Street
Hirokazu "Hero" Sakai worked at a McDonald's in Japan, where he was impressed with the fast-food system but not as much with the fast food. He wanted to use the system to sell a nutritious food. He had a conscience. This explains why his restaurant didn't become a chain. His food was the Japanese sweet potato, which is different from the common sweet potato, but not so that a person who loves a sweet potato would care. He trumpeted his food's health benefits, and after all, you weren't required to have your sweet potato with cinnamon sugar, maple syrup, or chocolate sauce. Besides the sweet potatoes, Hero's had sweet potato cream soup, sweet potato salad, and sweet potato pita sandwiches. I've disclosed my relationship with this place and its food in this section's introduction. I'll just add that this was the only non-dessert restaurant I could leave without craving dessert.

HOTPUFFS, was at 179 Madison Avenue
"HOTPUFFS are soft and fresh dough products," the menu announced, then promised: "They are all freshly baked or fried to your order." The Classic Puffs were the Stuffed Puffs, which came in rectangles, triangles, and crescents. They were called, respectively, Stuffed RecPuffs, Stuffed TriPuffs, and Stuffed CresPuffs. Stuffed RecPuffs were stuffed with stuff like mashed potatoes or chickpeas. Stuffed TriPuffs were stuffed with stuff like ricotta cheese and raisins. Stuffed CresPuffs were stuffed with stuff like chicken or ground beef. There were also TopPuffs, which were open-faced Puffs with the stuff on top of the Puff. Maybe it was the complexity; maybe it was the

geometry; maybe it was the use of the term "dough products." But despite an alternative menu choice of grilled challah rolls—which were called Toast Puffs—it wasn't that long before HOTPUFFS stuffed its last Puff.

JANE'S SWEET BUNS, was at 102 St. Mark's Place

The East Village is a mecca for people in search of spirits and snacks, so there was logic to a product that could appetizingly fuse the two. Jane's product was a line of pastries, all conveniently spiked with booze. Jane was a baker who, conveniently, was also a bartender. She sold sticky buns with bourbon, and cinnamon buns with rum, and raspberry tartlettes with gin, and Harvey Wallbanger cake. Her official concept was "pastries inspired by cocktails," and she thus gave her pastries names like the Frenchie and the Dark and Stormy. Understandably, the place got press, but it never seemed to take off. The product may not have been as logical as it seemed. It could be that Jane left her customers too thirsty for more, which could be why the store's owner shut her bake shop down and replaced it with a bar.

MY MAKI, was at 142 E. 43rd Street

UrbanDaddy called this the place to "brainstorm, micromanage and give birth to new versions of the handroll." No doubt they meant it as a compliment, but most likely, it's why My Maki was gone in a few months. Maybe most of us just don't want to give birth at lunch. Maybe most of us also don't have the obstetric skills to give birth to sushi, even when the process is laid out on a menu board in five steps. Those steps involved choosing from 2 wraps, 28 ingredients, 7 toppings, and 8 sauces. Most of us don't get that much time off for lunch. After brainstorming and micromanaging, you could give birth to, say, a soy-wrap eel roll with jalapeño, mango, sun-dried tomato, cream cheese, and Doritos—topped with crab mix and crunchy tempura, and dipped in citrus ponzu sauce. The step model may work in some places, but not in maki maternity.

TREAT PETITE, was at 61 Grove Street

Treat Petite's chief asset was that it sold frozen kefir. Its chief liability was also that it sold frozen kefir. The product was tasty, but scary. That could explain why the owners didn't name the place Frozen Kefir, though it couldn't explain why they named it Treat Petite. Frozen kefir is similar to frozen yogurt, except scary. It's familiar in places like Russia and Azerbaijan. To tempt Americans, the owners served it in flavors like pomegranate and caramelized pineapple, and in "Kefir Concoctions" like Key Lime Pie and Balsamic Strawberries & Cream. They also offered toppings like Oreo crumbs and Cap'n Crunch, and they made the inside of the store look like a nice sunny boardwalk. But perhaps people were challenged enough just to get past "kefir" without having to get past "Treat Petite," not to mention "Concoctions."

AND LET'S NOT FORGET . . .

Baguette Bar (was at 179 MacDougal Street): They served twice-toasted, kosher-style, panini-style, baguette-only sandwiches, which may have been tough to promote.

B-Bap Fusion Rice Bar (was at 830 Ninth Avenue): Even those appetized by a four-step bowl of rice may have been less appetized by Step 2: "Select Your Protein."

Cafetiny (was at 11 W. Eighth Street): The cafe was tiny because it sold little more than Turkish coffee. Perhaps its menu needed to be a little less tiny.

Cheesestick Factory (was at 410 E. 13th Street): Reportedly, this was indeed a place built on cheesesticks, which could explain why it eventually crumbled.

Dolce Vizio Tiramisù (was at 131 Christopher Street): If cupcakes could have so many stores of their own in New York, then couldn't tiramisu have one? Actually—no.

K! Pizzacone (was at 325 Fifth Avenue): Despite a sign that contended that "Pizza isn't flat anymore!!!" this place didn't make a compelling case for its being conical.

Kung Fu Bing (was at 189 E. Houston Street): A bing is a kind of pancake, and this Chinese chain meant to make it as common here as the taco, but it didn't.

Nooï Pasta To-Go (was at 370 Lexington Avenue): This four-step pasta place opened at the same time as Hello Pasta, which was just up the street. Both went down the tubes.

"The Original" New York Milkshake Co. (was at 37 St. Mark's Place): It tried selling milkshakes in many flavors, when perhaps just "the original" three were enough.

Pitaria (was at 230 Thompson Street): They served everything on pitas, which may have saddled them with much the same problem that may have sunk Baguette Bar.

Popover Café (was at 551 Amsterdam Avenue): This spot managed to work popovers into just about anything you chose from the menu. It worked for about 30 years.

PressToast (was at 112 MacDougal Street): PressToasts were essentially Israeli panini. It's possible that people just weren't psyched for za'atar.

Pure Dark (was at 350 Bleecker Street): Its "chocolate harvested from nature" may have been a little too precious, not to mention a little too dear.

U.S. Chips (was at Grand Central Terminal): Reportedly, this was a potato-chip stop that predated Chippery, and thus might have served as a warning.

Wechsler's Currywurst (was at 120 First Avenue): Bratwurst in ketchup has its own museum in Berlin, but it just couldn't get that kind of respect in New York.

THE ONE-*THING* HALL OF FAME

A&S BOOK, was at 304 W. 40th Street

Whenever the newsstand let you down, A&S loaded you up. Its confusing name notwithstanding, it was the mecca for magazines. It carried about a thousand titles, and stocked about two million copies. It had 1896 *Ladies' Home Journal*s and 1990 *Penthouse Forum*s. It had three floors packed with magazines, which it sold to collectors, designers, artists, movie studios, and people who really liked magazines. It had your *Field & Stream*, your *House & Garden*, your *Road & Track*, your *Town & Country*, your *Art & Antiques*, and your *U.S. News & World Report*. Through the years it changed owners, and it finally changed its name to the more suitable A&S Magazines. Now, like its stock, it's history. So now try to find a place where you can flip through the March 1935 *Modern Screen* with the headline "Jimmie Cagney Tells Girls How to Protect Themselves."

BIG CITY KITE CO., was at 1201 Lexington Avenue

It opened in 1963 with what was arguably a more New York–centric name: Go Fly a Kite. Despite changes not only in name but also in address and in ownership, it stayed aloft for 41 years, which is good for any store and nearly preposterous for a store that sells only kites. At most times it had well over a hundred different kites, from little plastic kiddie kites to big delta-wing stunt kites. It had single-line deltas and diamonds, dual-line deltas and diamonds, deltas with cats and dinosaurs, and diamonds with fish and flamingos. It kept kite addicts in kites and hooked new kiters on kites. The last owner, David Klein, told me that kiting lifted them all. "It calms you down," he said. "I had one customer who started flying kites and stopped seeing his psychiatrist. And he works on Wall Street."

JUST CATS, was at 244 E. 60th Street

Alison Steele was the Nightbird, but she nevertheless loved cats, so, with her sister, she opened a store that was devoted to cats. It sold actual cats, or at least kittens, as well as things for cats and kittens. It also sold cat things for people who were also devoted to cats. It had cat-themed clothing, cat-themed jewelry, cat-themed art, and cat-themed crafts. They were all upscale, like the things for cats, which included custom-made cat homes. "We don't carry kitschy cat things," Alison told the *New York Times*. "We carry quality items that happen to feature cats." Alison became the Nightbird as a late-night disc jockey in the early days of FM progressive rock radio. She whispered "Come, fly with me," which could be why her show attracted young men. Still, her company in the studio was not a man, a cat, or a bird, but rather Genya, who was a French poodle.

THE LAST WOUND-UP, was at 889 Broadway, 290 Columbus Avenue, and South Street Seaport

The byword of this wondrous shop was "Don't Postpone Joy," and you couldn't help but heed the advice from the moment you walked in. The place was decked with hundreds of wind-up things, including what the owner claimed was the world's biggest collection of wind-up toys. There were walking turtles, walking pineapples, and walking birthday cakes; there were splashing frogs, swimming penguins, hopping bunnies, and waddling ducks. There were classics like the Musical Monkey With Clashing Cymbals and, of course, the mandatory chattering teeth. The owner was Nathan Cohen, who also claimed that he had no choice but to open the store after he came up with the name. He showed off his wind-ups. He told jokes. He played Beethoven on a Pee Wee harmonica. "People who like toys," he told me, "are usually people who like life."

MAXILLA & MANDIBLE, was at 451 Columbus Avenue

A maxilla's an upper jawbone, a mandible's a lower jawbone, and the two of them got together to tell you that this was the city's bone store. You could buy a complete skeleton or bones à la carte, including skulls, including the signature Genuine New York City Rat Skull. The place billed itself as "the world's first and only osteological store." But along with bones and teeth, it carried fossils and insects. So along with osteologists, it supplied paleontologists and entomologists. It did things like designing museum exhibits, but it mostly kept people in touch with their framework. The store was founded in 1983 by Henry Galiano, who had worked at the American Museum of Natural History before running a flea-market skull booth. It closed in 2011, leaving a city full of disappointed teachers, artists, jewelers, filmmakers, and just plain good-natured ghouls.

ONLY HEARTS, still at 386 Columbus Avenue
Since the store is still there, why is it in the Hall of Fame? Because it was once a somewhat different store, even though it's the same one. While it has the same owner and name, it's now known mostly for its women's apparel. But when it opened in 1978, it carried what its name says—only hearts. It had heart-shaped pillows, buckets, birdcages, telephones, juggling balls, and fly swatters. It had heart-adorned tissues, trivets, matchboxes, pencils, padded hangers, and socks. It had trays to make heart-shaped ice cubes, wands to make heart-shaped bubbles, irons to make heart-shaped waffles, and punches to make heart-shaped holes. It still carries heart things, from soaps to paperweights, but it's evolved into less of a theme store than a fashion store. The clothes, however, include the owner's line of what she calls Inner Outerwear, which are clothes that are lacy and silky, which themselves can be good for the heart.

RECORDS REVISITED, was at 34 W. 33rd Street
Lots of record stores have closed. In fact, most record stores have closed. But this particular record store was not like most. This one sold only records that played at 78 rpm—the kind of records you probably couldn't play even if you could still play records. Morty Savada got out of pajamas, which he'd been selling for 30 years, to sell records that had been obsolete for two decades before he sold them. He stocked around 200,000, dating from the 1890s to the 1960s. He had whistling records, yodeling records, laughing

records, and sneezing records. He spent a lot of time filing and retrieving records, but he was always happy to take a few minutes to play you records. He died in 2008 and left his records to Syracuse University—giving it the largest collection of 78s after the Library of Congress.

SEASHELLS UNLIMITED, was at 590 Third Avenue

Veronica Parker Johns was not only the president of Seashells Unlimited, but also, at least in 1975, the president of the New York Shell Club. In her oceanic shop she sold, as advertised, unlimited seashells, along with such reasonable ancillaries as coral and shark's teeth. She also came out of her shells. For 42 years she was an active member of the Mystery Writers of America. She turned out books with names like *Shady Doings* and *The Singing Widow*, and wrote stories that made it to TV series like *The Alfred Hitchcock Hour*. Her store was one of those tiny ones that can make you feel confined, but when it was open she was usually in it, to help you fulfill your shell needs. She died in 1988, but fortunately not before writing the book she was surely born to write. It was called *She Sells Seashells*.

THINK BIG!, was at 390 W. Broadway and 313 Columbus Avenue

This was the place that made it possible for you to pay $18 for an aspirin, and that was back in the '80s, when that figure was high. But it was a 7-inch-wide aspirin, which was exactly what you needed after trying to screw in the 2-foot-tall lightbulb for which you paid $195. Since the store had an outsized stock, it was suggestively called Think Big! It brought a whole new dimension to the term "extra large." It had a 3-foot safety pin for $25, a 5-foot crayon for $40, and a 20-inch bottle of Heinz Tomato Ketchup for $70, with no ketchup. These and things like them were purchased as wry decor and gifts. Some of them were functional, such as the lightbulb, which was a lamp. They made it into the homes of big names—and into big movies, like *Big*—but even the biggest things apparently can't stay big forever.

UNCLE SAM, was at 161 W. 57th Street

Uncle Sam was an umbrella institution. It had not only umbrellas, but every-thing to do with umbrellas. It made, caned, recovered, and monogrammed umbrellas. It opened in 1866 and lasted well over 125 years. The store was owned by the same family for generations and had several branches. It also carried canes, but other than that, it was all umbrellas. Needless to say, it carried every size, style, and caliber of umbrellas. Needless to say, that included some bold ideas in umbrellas. "We had the hat umbrella," Gilbert Center, a store manager, told me. "We had the radio umbrella. . . . We had the lamp umbrella. . . . We had the dog umbrella. It attached to the collar of the dog. I took it home and tried it on one of my own dogs. He got so scared, he wouldn't go out of the house."

AND LET'S NOT FORGET. . .

After the Rain (was at 149 Mercer Street): This was a kaleidoscope store. It was around in the '90s, when there was actually a kaleidoscope boom.

Altar Egos (was at 110 W. Houston Street): It sold altars, rather than egos, though what you did at your altar was your business.

Amethyst (was at 32 E. Seventh Street): This store actually had many differ-ent things. The thing is, all of them were purple.

The Ballet Shop (was at 1887 Broadway): The Ballet Shop sold most types of ballet memorabilia, yet curiously didn't sell leotards, slippers, or tutus.

Be a Doll (was at 99 Prince Street): With a photograph, Audrey Rubin could put your face on a rag doll. This could appeal either to your vanity or to your humility.

Beta Only (was at 202 W. 49th Street): For a while, there was a duel between two kinds of videocassettes—VHS and Betamax. Betamax lost.

Bottles Unlimited (was at 245 E. 78th Street): Not only was this a store that sold antique bottles, but it had an owner, William Delafield, who was known as "Bottle Bill."

Everything Angels (was at 9 W. 31st Street): This store actually had many different things. The thing is, all of them sported angels.

Fizzazz (was at 280 Columbus Avenue): It sold Coca-Cola clothing. For Coca-Cola souvenirs, you went to Coca-Cola Fifth Avenue, which also fizzled.

Mariposa (was at South Street Seaport): Billed as "The Butterfly Gallery," it dealt in art made of dead butterflies. Reportedly, like its subjects, it died a natural death.

Modern Stone Age (was at 54 Greene Street): Its name intentionally linked it to *The Flintstones*, which was appropriate since everything it sold was made out of rock.

Panoramics (was at 189 Broadway and on Bleecker Street): Panoramics were unusually wide photographs, and thus perhaps not the best art form for the age of downsizing.

Rita Ford Music Boxes (was at 19 E. 65th Street): Rita sold both old and new music boxes. She died in 1993, but her business lives on in New Jersey.

See Hear (was at 33 St. Mark's Place): In the '90s this was the world head-quarters for zines. These days zines are not in need of world headquarters.

Under Wares (was at 210 E. 58th Street): It was more or less a lingerie store for men. There was another one called Underworld. Both were probably undersold.

APPENDIX A: ONE-FOOD WONDERS BY FOOD

APPENDIX B: ONE-FOOD WONDERS BY NEIGHBORHOOD

Battery Park
Little Muenster, 51

Chelsea
Artichoke Basille's Pizza, 146
Beyond Sushi, 12
Doughnut Plant, 28, 33
Fat Witch Bakery, 149
Go! Go! Curry!, 151
Lasagna Ristorante, 153
The Meatball Shop, 29, 66
Tuck Shop, 134

East Harlem
Dough Loco, 148

East Village
Artichoke Basille's Pizza, 146
Caracas Arepa Bar, 18, 27
Crif Dogs, 24
Croissanteria, 127
Curry-Ya, 31
Empire Biscuit, 39
Gem Spa, 150
Luke's Lobster, 28, 54
The Nugget Spot, 186
Otafuku x Medetai, 81
Papaya King, 83
Porchetta, 104

Sakaya, 161
Schnitz, 113
Sigmund's Pretzels, 117
S'MAC, 119
Snowdays, 122
Tuck Shop, 134
Wafels & Dinges, 140

Financial District
Go! Go! Curry!, 151
Luke's Lobster, 28, 54

Flatiron
Melt Shop, 156

Gramercy
Beyond Sushi, 12

Greenwich Village
Artichoke Basille's Pizza, 146
Go! Go! Curry!, 151
The Kati Roll Company, 45
La Frite, 152
Manousheh, 154
Meatball Obsession, 63
Meltkraft, 29, 156
OatMeals, 78
100 Montaditos, 158
Peanut Butter & Co., 86
Pommes Frites, 99

INDEX

ABOUT THE AUTHOR

Mitch Broder is the author of *Discovering Vintage New York*, the first and only guide to the city's classic restaurants, shops, bars, and nightspots. He covered New York City as a feature writer and columnist for Gannett Newspapers, the nation's largest newspaper chain.

He has also written for papers including the *New York Times*, the *Washington Post*, and the *Los Angeles Times*. Among his journalism awards are the Mike Berger Award from Columbia University and the Best Humorous Writing Award from the Society of the Silurians.

PRAISE FOR MITCH BRODER'S
DISCOVERING VINTAGE NEW YORK

"A nostalgia-lover's guide, *Discovering Vintage New York* not only recalls some of the city's favorite restaurants and other hangouts but also reveals the people behind them."
—Sam Roberts, *New York Times*

"Mitch Broder is a journalist who is well aware of the transience of 'vintage' New York. Even the places that you assume will be around forever can one day disappear. But this fun little book celebrates the classic New York restaurants, shops and nightclubs . . . places that form the heart of the city."
—June Sawyers, *Chicago Tribune*

"In an age when Times Square feels like Disney World and Manhattan is overrun by chain stores and franchise coffee houses, Broder takes readers to locales where the quirky charm of old New York still thrives."
—Richard Liebson, Gannett Newspapers

"Mitch Broder respects his elders: venerable chop houses, hot dog stands with aged neon signs, timeworn diners, classic bookstores."
—Chris Erikson, *New York Post*

"*Discovering Vintage New York* is a must-have guide to what remains—before it vanishes."
—Jeremiah Moss, *Jeremiah's Vanishing New York*

"If you long for a time forgotten and a guide to the bygone metropolis, read *Discovering Vintage York*. Your next visit to the Big Apple could be an unforgettable one."
—Cristine Struble, Examiner.com

"Hillary and I are delighted to have a copy."
—Bill Clinton, former president of the United States